THE COFFEE ROASTER'S COMPANION

Scott Rao

Experience without theory is blind,
but theory without experience is mere intellectual play.

—paraphrase of Immanuel Kant

Liz Clayton and I thank Cafe Grumpy, Stone Street Coffee, Gillies Coffee Company, Pulley Collective, Intelligentsia Coffee, Irving Farm Coffee Roasters, and Dallis Bros. Coffee for graciously allowing her to photograph their roasting facilities for this book.

The author has taken care in preparation of this book but assumes no responsibility for errors or inaccuracies.

ISBN 978-1-4951-1819-7

Text and graphics copyright 2014 by Scott Rao
Photographs copyright 2014 by Liz Clayton

Photography by Liz Clayton
Book design by Rebecca S. Neimark, Twenty-Six Letters

Please visit www.scottrao.com for information about purchasing this book.

Table of Contents

Acknowledgments

I'm grateful to several talented people for their help in creating this book. I would not have written a chapter on green coffee without Ryan Brown's help. Ryan's patient tutoring and vast knowledge of green coffee are responsible for most of the green-coffee information contained here.

Andy Schecter, Rich Nieto, Ian Levine, Mark Winick, Liz Clayton, and Vince Fedele provided valuable edits and feedback on the first draft. Eric Svendson and Henry Schwartzberg generously offered their expertise on thermocouples. Liz Clayton created this book's lovely photos and contributed insightful editorial feedback. Janine Aniko converted my amateur drawings into professional graphics.

Rebecca Neimark is responsible for this book's handsome design and layout. Jean Zimmer, my editor and coach, cleaned up my cliché-laden prose and again made me look like a better writer than I am. I can't imagine publishing a book without those two.

James Marcotte's brilliant roasting turned me into a coffee lover two decades ago and set a standard that few roasters have since met.

Preface

Coffee roasting has always been something of a dark art. Although people have been roasting coffee for hundreds of years, little prescriptive or scientific writing about roasting exists. At best, roasters learn their trade by apprenticing under an experienced, competent roaster. More commonly, young roasters learn by trial and error, roasting and tasting countless batches, and develop a system based on folklore and spurious reasoning.

I spent the first ten years of my roasting career lost in the labyrinth of trial and error, and while I made some progress, it was usually of the "two steps forward, one step back" type. I desperately wanted a rational basis for my roasting beliefs, one that would prove itself in blind taste tests and apply to all beans and roasting machines.

After owning two roasting companies, I have had the good fortune to work as a consultant for many roasters. Through consulting I have had the opportunity to use many *coffee-roasting machines* and witness a variety of approaches to roasting and tasting. As part of my consulting work, I have often spent long hours analyzing roast data, trying to help my clients quantify their best practices. About six years ago I began to notice that the data of the rare, extraordinary batches all shared certain patterns, regardless of the bean or machine. I've spent the past six years testing and refining those patterns; they form the foundation of the system I present in this book.

I don't claim to have all, or even most, of the answers. Despite my ignorance, I offer the ideas in this book to begin a long-overdue conversation about how to systematically roast coffee. Merely claiming that coffee roasting should be subjected to a systematic, objective, evidence-based approach is sure to offend some coffee professionals. Many roasters believe their special "feel" for roasting makes their coffee great. However, as recent technological advances have improved our ability to measure roast *development* and consistency, those "intuitive" roasters' results have usually been found lacking.

With the introduction of data-logging software and the coffee *refractometer,* roasters have powerful new tools to track and measure results, making the process more predictable and consistent. I confess I miss the romance of making countless manual adjustments during a roast, furiously scribbling notes in a logbook, and running back and forth between the machine and logbook fifty times per batch. Watching a *roast profile's* progress on a computer screen lacks the visceral satisfaction of the old methods. I don't roast for my own entertainment, however; I roast to give my customers the best-tasting coffee I can. On the rare occasion when I allow myself to sit quietly and enjoy a coffee, I'm grateful for the results.

Introduction

This book is meant to be a reference for any roaster, whether a beginner or a professional. For our purposes, I will focus on *light*-to-*medium* roasting of *specialty coffee* processed in a batch *drum roaster* in 8–16 minutes. Most of what I will discuss also applies to *continuous roasters, high-yield roasters, fluid-bed roasters,* and other roasting technologies. However, I will not often refer to such roasting machines directly.

I implore the reader to study this entire book and not focus solely on the "how to" chapters. Experience with my previous books has taught me that readers who cherry-pick the parts that appeal to them end up missing some of the big picture, leading them to misapply some recommendations. I've italicized potentially unfamiliar terms throughout the text and defined them in the glossary at the end of the book.

THE COFFEE ROASTER'S COMPANION

Why We Roast Coffee Beans

Coffee beans are the seeds of the *cherries* of the coffee tree. Each cherry typically contains two beans whose flat sides face each other. When steeped in hot water, raw, or "green," coffee beans offer little in the way of what one might relate to as coffee *taste* and *aroma*.

Roasting green coffee creates myriad chemical changes, the production and breakdown of thousands of compounds, and, the roaster hopes, the development of beautiful *flavors* when the beans are ground and steeped in hot water. Among its many effects, roasting causes beans to

- Change in color from green to yellow to tan to brown to black.
- Nearly double in size.
- Become half as dense.
- Gain, and then lose, sweetness.
- Become much more *acidic*.
- Develop upwards of 800 aroma compounds.
- Pop loudly as they release pressurized gases and water vapor.

The goal of roasting is to optimize the flavors of coffee's *soluble chemistry*. Dissolved solids make up brewed coffee's taste, while dissolved *volatile aromatic compounds* and oils are responsible for aroma.[20] Dissolved solids, oils, and suspended particles, primarily fragments of bean *cellulose,* create coffee's *body*.[20]

It's important to pick coffee cherries when ripe to maximize sweetness and acidity.

Coffee beans covered in mucilage from inside the cherry.

▪ 2 ▪
Green-Coffee Chemistry

R aw coffee beans are dense, green seeds consisting of about one-half carbohydrate in various forms and one-half a mixture of water, proteins, lipids, acids, and *alkaloids*. Roasters do not need to know much about green coffee's chemistry to roast delicious coffee, but I offer the following summary to familiarize readers with the primary components of green coffee.

Structure

A raw coffee bean's structure is a three-dimensional cellulose, or polysaccharide, matrix containing approximately a million cells.[10] Coating the cellulose strands within that matrix are hundreds of chemicals that the roasting process will transform into the oils and soluble material that determine brewed coffee's flavor. Green coffee's cellulose structure contributes half of its dry weight.[5] The cellulose contributes little to coffee flavor but does trap some volatile compounds, which are responsible for aroma, and adds to brewed coffee's viscosity, increasing its perceived body.[5]

Sugars

Sugars, dominated by sucrose, make up 6%–9% of a green bean's dry weight* and provide sweetness in the cup. Sucrose also contributes to development of acidity, as the *caramelization* of sucrose during roasting yields acetic acid.[2]

Lipids

Lipids, primarily triglycerides, make up approximately 16% of green coffee's dry weight.[5] Although lipids are not water soluble, brewed coffee contains some, especially when the brewing method uses either no filtration (e.g., *cupping)* or a very porous filter (e.g., espresso, French press, or metal- or cloth-filter drip). Lipids in brewed coffee help retain aroma and contribute to coffee's *mouthfeel.* Higher lipid content is generally associated with better green-coffee quality.[3] Unfortunately, lipids also present challenges to quality, as they are vulnerable to oxidation and rancidity during storage of roasted beans.

Proteins

Proteins and free amino acids make up 10%–13% of green coffee by dry weight.[3] Amino acids and *reducing sugars* in coffee beans interact during roasting in

---

* Data on green-coffee composition refers to the genus *Coffea* species *arabica* only. The chemical compositions of *Coffea robusta* and other species of coffee differ, sometimes significantly, from that of *arabica.*

nonenzymatic browning reactions known as *Maillard reactions.* These reactions produce glycosylamines and melanoidins[18] that contribute to coffee's bittersweet flavor, brown color, and roasted, meaty, and baked aromas.

Alkaloids: Caffeine and Trigonelline

Two alkaloids, *caffeine* and *trigonelline,* each account for approximately 1% of green coffee's dry weight and are responsible for much of coffee's *bitterness* and stimulating properties. Caffeine contributes approximately 10% of coffee's bitterness and the majority of its stimulant effect. The coffee plant produces caffeine as a defense against consumption by insects.[7] A coffee tree planted at a high altitude would probably produce beans with less caffeine because of the lower risk of insect attack.

Trigonelline is perhaps the greatest contributor to coffee's bitterness, yields many aromatic compounds, and degrades to pyridines and nicotinic acid during roasting.[3] Nicotinic acid is also known as niacin, or vitamin B_3; a mere 7 oz (200 g) of brewed coffee, depending on roast degree, contains 20–80 ml of niacin,[26] which is likely responsible for coffee's documented anti-cavity effect.[25]

Moisture Content

Ideally, water should account for 10.5%–11.5% of green-coffee weight. If moisture content is too low, bean color is typically faded and the cup has notes of hay and straw. A roaster must apply heat cautiously to low-moisture beans, as they are likely to roast too fast. If moisture content is much higher than 12%, green coffee is prone to developing mold and may taste grassy in the cup. Water slows heat transfer within beans,[8] and it requires extra heat input to evaporate. Roasting very moist beans therefore requires extra energy in some combination of added time and roasting power.

Organic Acids

Organic acids, primarily *chlorogenic acids* (CGAs), constitute approximately 7%–10% of green coffee's dry mass. CGAs contribute to coffee's acidity, sourness, *astringency,* and bitterness. Robusta coffee's higher CGA content is likely responsible for its significantly greater bitterness. For both the coffee bean and the coffee drinker, CGAs offer antioxidant benefits.[38] Other organic acids in coffee include citric, quinic, caffeic, malic, acetic, and formic.

Gases and Aromatics

Volatile aromatic compounds provide coffee's aroma. Green coffee contains more than 200 volatiles but offers little aroma. Roasting creates the vast majority of coffee's aromatic compounds, and so far, researchers have identified over 800 volatiles in roasted coffee.[8]

▪ 3 ▪

Green-Coffee Processing and Storage

This chapter was cowritten by Ryan Brown.

Green-coffee processing affects cup quality as well as how one should roast beans. Once a bean has been processed, a roaster must carefully control its packaging and storage conditions to prevent degradation of quality before it's roasted.

Primary Processing Methods

Washed, natural, and pulped natural are the three primary processing methods of specialty coffee.

Wet/Washed

The washed, or wet, process consists of the following steps:

1. Pulping of the cherry to remove the skin.
2. Removal of the sticky mucilage layer by fermentation or mechanical means.
3. Washing of the beans to remove loosened mucilage.
4. Drying of the beans in parchment, either mechanically for 1–2 days or in the sun for 3–16 days.

Dry/Natural

The natural, or dry, process consists of partially or completely drying the coffee cherries on the tree and then husking the cherries to remove their skins. Alternatively, the cherries are picked when ripe and then dried before husking.

Pulped/Natural

In the pulped/natural process, the cherries are pulped to remove their skin and set to dry with the mucilage layer intact. This method delivers a sweeter, cleaner cup than does the traditional natural process.

Washed processing produces cleaner, more acidic, more consistent, and generally more-prized coffee than natural processing does. Washed coffees also tend to be denser and require more aggressive roasting. The dry process can take several weeks and yields coffee with less acidity, more body, and earthier flavors than washed coffee. Arid growing areas often use the natural process because it requires much less water than the washed process. Natural-processed coffees burn more easily during roasting, so one should use lower *charge temperatures* and gas settings when roasting those beans.

Green-Coffee Storage

Until recent years, all coffee was packaged in *burlap* (jute) sacks and shipped in containers, arriving at roasters months after the coffee was processed. Roasters and importers frequently had the experience of cupping a coffee at origin, and perhaps cupping and approving a "pre-shipment sample," only to receive coffee ruined by exposure to poor atmospheric conditions in storage or in transit.

In the past ten years, several small, quality-driven roasters have spearheaded a revolution in green-coffee packaging and transport. Many roasting companies, even some of the smallest ones, now buy coffee directly from farmers, share cupping and green-grading information with the farmers, and demand speedy delivery of coffee in packaging designed to preserve its freshness and quality. Such packaging is costly but justified, given the ever-increasing premiums paid for specialty coffees.

The following is a survey of the more prominent packaging options:

Burlap (jute) bags are the most common and economical option for packaging and transporting green coffee. Jute is a renewable resource, and the bags are cheap; their use requires no special skills or equipment beyond those that are standard at any dry mill or exporting operation. Burlap sacks do not protect coffee from moisture or odors, however, so the coffee is vulnerable to damage during transport and storage.

Burlap bags are the most economical option for packaging and transporting green coffee.

Both vacuum-sealed bags (left photo) and GrainPro bags (right photo) protect beans from moisture and odors.

Vacuum sealing is the best available packaging for green coffee. Vacuum-sealed bags protect beans from moisture, odors, and oxygen, dramatically slowing the *respiration,* and therefore the aging, of green coffee. Before vacuum sealing, care must be taken to measure beans' *water activity* to prevent development of mold during storage. Vacuum packaging costs approximately USD 0.15–0.25 per pound (EUR 0.45–0.75 per kilogram), requires special equipment and skill to implement, and often delays shipment of green coffee, so it is not without its costs and risks.

GrainPro and other *hermetically* sealed bags protect coffee against moisture and odors and are cheaper and easier to use than vacuum packaging. GrainPro bags preserve coffee significantly longer than burlap sacks but perhaps half as long as vac-sealed bags do. At a cost of about USD 0.05–0.10 per pound (EUR 0.15–0.30 per kilogram), GrainPro bags are often the best and most practical option for quality-conscious roasters. As with vacuum sealing, to prevent development of mold and other microorganisms during storage, it is important to measure beans' water activity before packaging them in GrainPro bags.

Freezing—that is, storing green coffee in vacuum-sealed bags at a temperature below 32°F (0°C)—preserves flavor almost perfectly for years. Some roasters freeze special lots of beans and offer them as "vintage" coffees years after harvest, but there is not much consumer demand for such coffees at the moment. While it's impressive to experience five-year-old beans that taste as good as last month's crop, freezing is expensive and, arguably, wasteful. Freezing is an alternative worth considering in hot climates, however, as storage in extreme heat for a few days will ruin most green coffees.

Regardless of the packaging type she chooses, a roaster should take steps to ensure that her warehouse provides stable storage conditions all year round. Excessively warm or humid conditions; storing beans high off the ground, where the temperature may be hotter than realized; and storing beans too close to a hot roasting machine can all degrade green-coffee quality.

Water Activity and Moisture Content

Water activity (a_w) is a measure of the strength of the bond between water and the dry material of a coffee bean or other food product. (Please refer to the glossary, at the end of the book, for a more technical definition.) The a_w level indicates how likely moisture is to migrate into or out of a bean, which in turn affects how beans interact with their storage environment and how fast they degrade during storage.

Water activity differs from moisture content, which is the percentage, by weight, of water in green coffee. The two measures correlate, though their correlation may decrease when moisture content rises above 12%. Both characteristics influence cup quality, the degradation rate of green coffee during storage, and the risk of microbial growth during storage.

I am not aware of formal research into what a_w levels correlate most with cup quality. An informal poll of importers and green buyers I admire suggests that the optimum a_w level ranges between 0.53 and 0.59. The ideal range of moisture contents is better established: Based on my experience, I recommend that roasters acquire green coffee having a moisture content of 10.5%–11.5%. Choosing a green coffee with a_w and moisture content in those ranges and storing it in a stable environment of perhaps 68°F–72°F (20°C–22°C) and 45%–50% relative humidity should offer optimal conditions for stabilizing quality. Beans in hermetically sealed bags may benefit from colder storage temperatures but should be warmed to room temperature for several days before roasting.

Relation Between Water Activity and Moisture (Colombia Samples 2013)

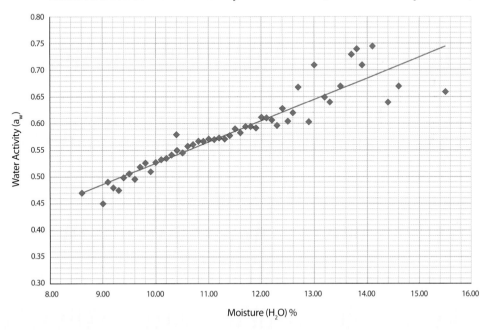

This graph shows the breakdown in the correlation of water activity and moisture content for beans having a moisture content above 12% (reproduced by gracious permission from Virmax Café).

Seasonality

In recent years, roasters have emphasized offering only coffees that are "in season." Like much else in the coffee industry, there is no consensus definition of seasonality. Some consider a coffee to be seasonal if it is from the most recent harvest, while others define seasonality based on an arbitrary amount of time elapsed since harvest.

I offer a definition of seasonality in the words of my friend Ryan Brown, an expert green buyer: "We care about seasonality because we care about cup quality. A coffee should be considered seasonal so long as the cup is vibrant, shows structured acidity, and is free of any signs of 'age' (such as paperiness, 'bagginess,' dryness, loss of organic material, etc.). It doesn't need to be any more complicated than that."

Physical Changes During Roasting

R oasting causes beans to change color, lose moisture, expand, and become brittle. While all professionals label roast levels based on bean color, there is no consensus on exactly what roast level each name indicates.

Color Changes

The first stage of roasting is commonly known as the "drying phase," although beans lose moisture at similar rates throughout most of the roasting process. During the first few minutes of roasting, degradation of chlorophyll causes beans to change color from green to yellow. As roasting progresses, the beans change from yellow to tan to light brown, primarily due to Maillard reactions. Late in a roast, as the beans approach *first crack,* the brown color deepens due to caramelization. In a dark roast, *carbonization* may turn beans black.

Classic Definitions of Roast Degree

These beans were photographed at 1-minute intervals during preparation of a French roast.

During roasting, coffee beans change from green to yellow to tan to brown, and, if roasted very dark, black. No universal system exists for naming different degrees of roast; what one roaster calls a "light roast" another roaster may label "full city."

Light roasts offer acidic, floral, and fruity flavors, more delicate aroma, and less body than *dark roasts*. Dark roasts develop smoky, *pungent*, bitter, and carbonized flavors. If one takes roasting to an extreme, burnt flavors dominate and body declines.

The coffee industry's lack of an agreed-upon nomenclature for degrees of roast causes confusion among roasters and consumers alike. I don't claim to offer the "correct" definitions for different roast levels, but I believe the following descriptors represent common and reasonable interpretations of various roast degrees and bean colors.

Cinnamon

Cinnamon* roasts are generally _dropped,_ that is, discharged from the roaster, sometime very early in first crack. Few consumers desire the green, grassy, often "peanutty" flavors of a cinnamon roast. However, some larger companies selling beans to cost-conscious consumers favor the very low *weight loss* of cinnamon roasts.

In the cup: Very acidic, often "green" or "peanutty," with grassy and floral aromas and very light body.

Cinnamon roast

City roast

City

City roasts are those dropped during the last stages of, or just after, first crack. Such roasts produce light-bodied coffee with very high acidity. City roasts are the current fashion among more progressive, or third-wave**, roasters and have historically been the standard in Nordic countries.

---

* "Cinnamon" relates to the color of the beans at this roast level and has nothing to do with the flavor of cinnamon.

**Coffee importer Timothy Castle coined the term "third wave" in 2000 in reference to a movement refocusing on coffee quality. Castle described the first wave as the emergence of pioneering, quality-obsessed coffee entrepreneurs in the 1960s, '70s, and '80s who offered the first modern alternatives to large, institutional roasters. The second-wavers were a

In the cup: Acidic, winey, sweet (especially if developed well), and juicy, with floral and fruity aromatics, hints of caramel, and light body. Can be grassy, lemony, and tart if not developed adequately.

Full City

Roasts discharged just before *second crack* and the appearance of surface oils are known as *full city roasts*. Many consumers prefer full city roasts because they offer a pleasing balance of moderate acidity, mellow caramels, and medium body.

In the cup: Caramelly, with ripe fruit and medium body.

Full city roast

Viennese roast

Viennese

Viennese roasts are those dropped in the early moments of second crack, when oil has just begun to migrate to bean surfaces. The standard roast degree offered by Starbucks Corporation is an example of a darker Viennese roast.*

In the cup: Bittersweet, caramelly, pungent, and often nutty or spicy, with heavy, syrupy body.

---

group of skilled businesspeople in the '80s and '90s who offered quality coffee but were more business savvy and profit oriented than the first-wavers. The third wave developed as a rebellion against the compromises of the second wave and offers a renewed commitment to coffee quality. Common usage of "third wave" has evolved away from Castle's original definition and now typically refers to companies favoring lighter roasts and brewed-to-order coffee made by hipsters.

* I think of full city and Viennese roasts as the "crowd pleasers," though most connoisseurs and third-wave companies frown upon such roasts. Critics contend that a lighter roast highlights a bean's uniqueness, while a full city or darker roast blunts too much of a coffee's acidity and delicacy.

French roast   Italian roast

French

French roast indicates oily beans with pungent, bittersweet, and carbonized flavors. Such a dark roast makes it difficult to detect a bean's unique character.

In the cup: Burnt, bitter, and smoky, with hints of caramel; body may be heavy or medium, as body peaks at a lighter French roast and declines with further roasting.

Italian

Most Italian roasters drop their coffees at medium roasts, but somehow the darkest, oiliest, and most bitter and carbonized roast level has come to be known as *Italian roast*. Almost all Italian roasts are rancid by the time they are consumed because their degraded cellulose structures allow rapid oxidation and staling.

In the cup: Burnt, smoky, rancid, and carbonized, with medium body.

Structural Changes

The microstructure of green coffee is relatively organized and dense, with oils coating the cellulose matrix.[10] As coffee roasts, the generation of steam and carbon dioxide (CO_2) increases pressure within the beans, forcing their structure to expand and pores to enlarge. A couple of minutes before first crack, beans expand enough to begin freeing the silver-colored skin, or *chaff,* trapped within the folds of their center cracks. When the cellulose can stretch no farther, fissures form within beans and on their surfaces, violently expelling water vapor and gases, creating the popping noises of first crack.

Specialty roasters seeking a light or medium roast typically drop beans between the end of first crack and the beginning of second crack. After first crack, gas production continues, rebuilding pressure within the bean cells. Simultaneously, the bean structure becomes more brittle, setting the stage for second crack. While the primary cause of first crack is the buildup of steam pressure, accumulation of CO_2 is the main driver of second crack. Just before or after the onset of second crack, oils bleed to the bean surfaces; almost all roasters would regard this as an objective indicator of a dark roast.

Beans dropped during second crack. Note the surface oils and fissures.

Inner-Bean Development

Bean expansion and the release of water vapor and gases during the cracking phases weaken beans' cellulose structures and make them more porous and brittle. The darker, more porous, and more brittle the inner beans are, the more developed they are. Sufficient inner-bean development is a prerequisite for great grind quality, high extraction, and elimination of undesirable savory flavors.

Inner-bean development lags behind outer-bean development during roasting. A roaster must skillfully manage the process to ensure that the inner bean is sufficiently roasted by the time the outer bean reaches its intended color. Ideally, the final "spread," or color difference, between the inner and outer bean should be negligible in a light roast. The darker the roast, the larger the acceptable spread, provided the inner bean has developed to a certain minimum degree. Throughout this book, I will discuss strategies to optimize inner-bean development.

Bean Size, Density, and Weight Loss

Coffee loses 12%–24% of its weight during roasting, depending on initial moisture content, roast degree, and inner-bean development during roasting. The lightest palatable roasts are probably those dropped during the latter stages of first crack and typically have weight loss, or *shrinkage,* of 11%–13%.* About 30 seconds after first crack ends, shrinkage is roughly 14%–16%, while at the onset of second crack, shrinkage is around 17%–18%. Dark, oily roasts may have shrinkage of 22% or more. The light roasts currently popular in the specialty industry lose an average of 14%–16% of their initial weight.

In a light roast, water accounts for up to 90% of the lost weight. The rest is organic matter, primarily CO_2, as well as small amounts of chaff, carbon monoxide, nitrogen, volatile aromatic compounds, and volatile acids. Organic losses increase significantly with darker roasting: Organic-matter loss is 5%–8% in medium roasts and as high as 12% in very dark roasts.[5] As beans lose weight during roasting, they also expand to 150%–190% of their original volume. The simultaneous loss of weight and gain in volume equates to a density loss of almost half.

The *trowel* allows a roaster to sample beans during a roast.

---

* These estimates assume a green-coffee moisture content of 10%–12% and a roast time of 11–12 minutes. Actual shrinkage may vary considerably.

· 5 ·

Roasting Chemistry

To a coffee lover, the roasting process is nothing short of magic: Dense, dull-tasting green beans morph into ambrosial brown beans that release an intoxicating fragrance. During roasting, countless reactions, including Maillard reactions and caramelization, brown the beans and create hundreds of new taste and aroma compounds. The roasting process also conveniently makes the beans brittle enough to grind easily and porous enough to allow water to access and extract their soluble flavors.

Changes in Chemical Composition

A little more than one-third of roasted coffee, by weight, is water soluble. Proper brewing extracts approximately 19%–22% of roasted coffee's mass (or about 55%–60% of its soluble material, plus a tiny amount of lipids and cellulose fragments known as *fines).*

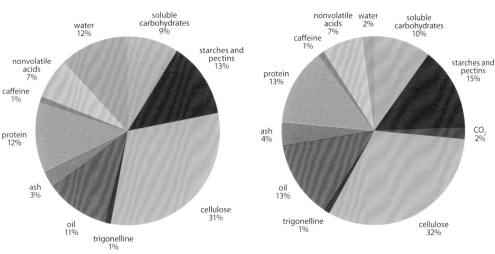

Green Coffee Bean Composition

water 12%
soluble carbohydrates 9%
nonvolatile acids 7%
starches and pectins 13%
caffeine 1%
protein 12%
ash 3%
oil 11%
trigonelline 1%
cellulose 31%

Roasted Coffee Bean Composition

nonvolatile acids 7%
water 2%
soluble carbohydrates 10%
caffeine 1%
protein 13%
starches and pectins 15%
ash 4%
CO_2 2%
oil 13%
trigonelline 1%
cellulose 32%

From this perspective, the most significant changes in bean composition during roasting are the loss of moisture from the bean (moisture drops from 12% to 2% of bean mass) and the development of CO_2 (from negligible to 2% of bean mass). The relevant amount of most dry components increase by 1 percentage point, due to water loss. Their weights don't change much during roasting, but their measure as a proportion of total bean weight increases. Please note: The numbers in the pie charts represent estimated norms; actual proportions will vary depending on the type of green coffee used, the roast degree, and other factors. (From Barter, R. (2004) A short introduction to the theory and practice of profile roasting. *Tea & Coffee Trade Journal.* 68, 34–37. Reprinted with permission from *Tea & Coffee Trade Journal.)*

Development of Acids During Roasting

Acidity gives coffee its liveliness, delicacy, complexity, and brightness. Although many coffee drinkers assume that acidity makes coffee bitter or unpleasant, coffee without acid is flat and boring. One can experience very low-acid coffee by brewing coffee with cold water for several hours. Such coffee can be smooth and chocolaty but lacks subtlety and becomes monotonous with regular consumption.

Chlorogenic acid (CGA) is by far the most prevalent acid in raw coffee beans, at 6%–8% of dry mass,[3] and coffee has the highest CGA content detected in any plant.[7] CGA contributes a great deal of brewed coffee's acidity and bitterness, as well as a minor stimulant effect.[10]

Roasting steadily breaks down CGA, with 50% remaining in a light roast and perhaps 20% in a dark roast.[2] CGA decomposes to quinic and caffeic acids, two astringent phenolic compounds that contribute body to coffee. In small amounts, quinic acid and caffeic acid contribute beneficial brightness and acidity[7] to coffee, but larger quantities produce undesirable levels of sourness and astringency.*

Coffee's other, minor organic acids also improve coffee flavor at low concentrations but produce undesirable flavors when out of balance. The concentrations of these acids generally increase and peak at a very light roast and decline steadily as roasting continues. The decrease in organic acids during roasting is what makes darkly roasted coffee less acidic than lightly roasted coffee.

Citric acid imparts sourness in coffee. In small quantities, acetic acid contributes a winey acidity but in large quantities yields a vinegary bitterness.[6] Malic acid contributes a clean, sour acidity and notes of apple.[6] Phosphoric acid, an inorganic acid found in high concentrations in Kenyan coffee, might be responsible for Kenya's unique and prized acidity.[6] Generally, the altitude at which a given coffee plant grows determines its beans' potential quantity of acidity, while its overall natural environment, and humidity in particular, is responsible for the types of acids it produces.[2]

When measuring coffee's acidity as pH, a lower pH value indicates higher acidity, and a higher value indicates lower acidity. Coffee bean acidity peaks sometime during first crack[11] and declines as roasting continues. The pH value of green coffee is approximately 5.8, decreases during roasting, and troughs (i.e., the level of acidity peaks) during first crack, at about 4.8, before steadily increasing with further roasting.[16] A combination of coffee's measurable acidity and particular balance of acids determines the *organoleptic* impression of its acidity. Therefore, a coffee drinker's perception of a brew's acidity is correlated with, but not identical to, its measurable acidity.

Raw coffee's sucrose content has a strong influence on its potential acidity and sweetness after roasting. Sucrose contributes to acidity because its caramelization yields acetic acid.[2] As such, it is critical that coffee growers harvest

---

* The breakdown of CGA also occurs in brewed coffee, particularly when the brewed coffee's temperature drops below 175°F (79°C). It is imperative to hold brewed coffee between 175°F–195°F (79°C–91°C) to stabilize CGA levels and limit the development of sour and astringent flavors.

Coffee cherries of varying ripeness. Riper beans contain more sucrose, which increases their potential sweetness and acidity in the cup.

coffee cherries when they are ripe because riper cherries yield beans with more sucrose. Darker roasting breaks down as much as 99% of sucrose, while light roasting degrades perhaps 87%.[37]

Aroma Development

The development of desirable aroma doesn't begin in earnest until several minutes into the roasting process. Rapid development of volatile aromatic compounds occurs at around the time bean moisture drops below 5%.[8] Caramelization and Maillard reactions, as well as degradation of amino acids, sugars, phenolic acids, and lipids, contribute to the development of aromatics.[8] Caramelization yields fruity, caramelly, nutty, and other aromas, while Maillard reactions produce savory, floral, chocolaty, earthy, and roasted aromas, among others.

The oils in coffee dissolve much of its volatile aromatic compounds and slowly release them as aroma during and after brewing.[8] Aroma content peaks at a light to medium roast. With further roasting, aroma destruction outpaces its creation, and aromatics become smokier and more pungent. Roasted beans gradually lose aroma during storage through outgassing. Darker roasts, with their weaker and more porous cellulose structures, lose aromatics more quickly than lighter roasts do.

Maillard Reactions and Caramelization

As noted, Maillard reactions are nonenzymatic browning reactions between free amino acids and reducing sugars, and they contribute to coffee's brown color, bittersweet flavor, and various aromas. Maillard reactions occur in the cooking of many foods, perhaps most familiarly in the browning of meats.

To understand the Maillard reactions' contribution to flavor, consider the different effects of roasting and boiling on the flavor of meat: Roasting imparts aromatics, complexity, and depth of flavor absent in boiled meats. Maillard reactions contribute similar roast-flavor traits and complexity to coffee beans.

During roasting, once a bean's internal temperature is high enough to boil off most of its moisture, the temperature rises more rapidly, speeding Maillard reactions. This is one reason aroma development accelerates at mid-roast. Maillard reactions become self-sustaining at above 320°F (160°C).

Unlike Maillard reactions, caramelization is a form of *pyrolysis,* or thermal decomposition. Caramelization begins at approximately 340°F (171°C),[19] as the heat of roasting breaks apart molecules of sugar and produces hundreds of new compounds, including smaller, bitter, sour, and aromatic molecules and larger, brown, flavorless molecules.[19] Although most people associate the word "caramel" with a very sweet dessert food, caramelization, ironically, decreases the sweetness and increases the bitterness of a food or beverage. Lighter roasts are sweeter, and darker roasts more bitter and caramelly, primarily because of caramelization.

Caffeine Content and Roasting

Despite what almost everyone has heard, darker roasting does not decrease the caffeine content of coffee beans. Caffeine levels are virtually unchanged by roasting,[3] as caffeine is stable at typical roasting temperatures. Given that beans lose mass during roasting, their proportion of caffeine by weight increases during roasting. Therefore, assuming one brews coffee of all roast degrees with a particular ratio of water to ground-coffee mass, rather than volume, darker roasts will yield brewed coffee with higher caffeine content.

▪ 6 ▪

Heat Transfer
in Coffee Roasting

Coffee roasting machines transfer heat to beans by *convection, conduction,* and *radiation*. Each roasting machine transfers heat by a different mix of these mechanisms. The following is an overview of how machine design affects heat transfer. I discuss roasting machine designs extensively in Chapter 7.

Convection, Conduction, and Radiation

"Classic" (my term) drum roasters, which apply heat directly to the drum, cook beans primarily by convection and secondarily by conduction. Radiant heating from hot roasting-machine surfaces and between neighboring beans makes a small contribution to heat transfer as well. In a personal communication with me, a representative of a well-known German manufacturer estimated heat transfer in his company's drum roasters to be 70% by convection and 30% by conduction.

Indirectly heated drum roasters segregate the drum from the heat source to maintain a cooler drum during roasting. Convection contributes a higher proportion of the heat transfer in these machines.

Fluid-bed roasters have no drum, and they roast by keeping the beans aloft in a high-velocity stream of hot gases. Recirculation roasters, such as the Loring Smart Roaster™, capture and reuse a proportion of the exhaust air from the roasting process. Both of these roasting machine designs transfer heat almost exclusively by convection.

At the beginning of a roast batch, charging the beans introduces a large volume of room-temperature beans and air into the hot roaster, sending the *environmental temperature* in the roaster plummeting. During the first few minutes of a batch in a classic drum roaster, conduction from the hot drum plays a significant role in transferring heat to the beans. As the air temperature in the roaster rebounds after its initial plunge, convection comes to dominate heat transfer. In such a machine the drum acts as a "heat-storage" device that jump-starts development early in a batch. Convection-oriented machines call for the use of hotter charge temperatures to provide adequate heat transfer early in a roast and compensate for lack of a heat-storing drum.

Heat Transfer and Temperature Gradient

The first two-thirds or so of roasting is an *endothermic* process, meaning the beans absorb energy, and heat is conducted from the outer bean to the inner bean. The *temperature gradient,* or "ΔT," within the beans largely determines the rate of heat transfer. Simply put, a

> Establishing a high ΔT early in a roast and minimizing it by the end of a roast is essential to creating good inner-bean development and a uniform roast.

Inner Vs. Outer Bean Temperature

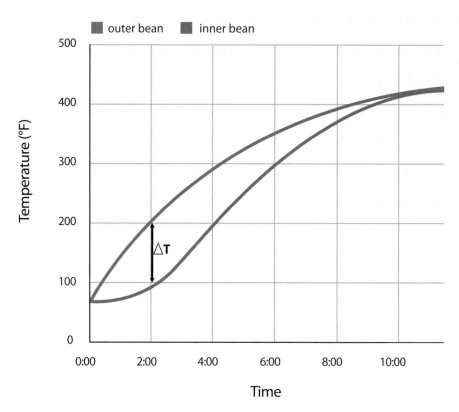

Note the large ΔT at 2:00.

greater ΔT causes more rapid heating of the inner bean. The ΔT early in a roast reaches an estimated 90°F (50°C),[10] peaks there or slightly higher, and decreases as roasting continues.* In other words, after the first few minutes of a roast, the bean-core temperature should slowly merge with the surface temperature as they both get hotter. In general, ΔT should peak higher in faster roasts and lower in longer roasts.

Heat and Mass Transfer Within Coffee Beans

Beginning at the outermost layer of a coffee bean, moisture evaporates during roasting and forms a "front of evaporation" that moves toward the bean's center.[5] The cellulose structure of the inner bean, being relatively cool, remains intact and traps moisture at the bean's core. The heating of this trapped water produces water vapor, increasing pressure within the bean and forcing its

---

* Very fast (2–3 minutes) roasts, such as those often used in laboratory experiments, may show significantly higher temperature gradients. Roast time and peak ΔT are negatively correlated; as the value of one increases, the value of the other decreases.

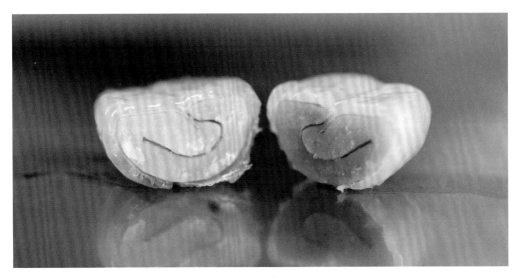

Cross section of a green coffee bean with mucilage layer.

structure to expand. This pressure, estimated by various researchers to peak as low as 5.4 atmospheres (550 kPa)[8] to as high as 25 atmospheres (2533 kPa),[18] builds until the stresses are great enough to disrupt the cellulose structure, at which point first crack occurs. Once the pressure, steam, and CO_2 escape during first crack, the bean's core temperature jumps.

Heat Transfer and Moisture

Both humidity in the roasting environment and moisture within beans influence heat transfer during roasting. After an initial lag, humidity in the roasting air increases the efficiency of heat transfer and causes faster moisture loss from the beans.[8] Moisture content within beans has a more complex influence on roasting. Greater moisture content has three major effects on heat transfer within a bean:

- It increases heat transfer because moisture increases a bean's thermal conductivity.
- It increases a bean's specific heat capacity, meaning that the bean requires more heat energy to raise its temperature by a given amount.
- It leads to greater transfer of evaporated moisture out of the bean, inhibiting heat transfer to the inner bean.

The net effect is that temperature rises more slowly in moister beans than in drier beans.[8] Therefore, machine operators should apply heat more aggressively when roasting moister beans and more judiciously when roasting drier beans.*

---

* I learned this lesson the hard way during my first winter as a roaster. My green coffee had lost much moisture during storage in that season's cold, dry air, and I found my coffees roasting too quickly. At first I didn't know why the beans were roasting so fast, but I learned to use less heat in my roasts that winter. The next autumn I installed a humidifier in the roastery and maintained constant temperature and humidity levels all year to stabilize the green coffee's moisture content.

· 7 ·
Roasting Machine Designs

A coffee-roasting machine is a specialized oven that transfers heat to coffee beans in a stream of hot gas while continually mixing the beans to ensure they roast evenly. Several types of roasters are in use today in the specialty coffee industry: classic drum roasters, indirectly heated drum roasters, fluid-bed roasters, recirculation roasters, and several others. Recirculation roasters return a portion of the exhaust air to the burner chamber to assist in heat generation for roasting. I will use the term "single-pass" to refer to machines that do not recirculate exhaust air. Each roaster design has distinct advantages and disadvantages, though no new design has eclipsed the popularity of the classic drum roaster, the design of which has not changed much in the past century.

Classic Drum

A classic drum roaster consists of a solid, rotating, cylindrical steel or iron drum laid horizontally on its axis, with an open flame below the drum. The flame heats both the drum and the air to be drawn through the drum. A fan draws hot gases from the burner chamber through the rotating beans and exhausts the smoke, steam, and various by-products of roasting and combustion out of the building through a vertical pipe, or "stack." The drum's rotation mixes the beans while they absorb heat by conduction from direct contact with the hot drum and convection from the air flowing through the drum.

At the completion of a roast, the machine operator opens the door to the drum, dumping the beans into the cooling bin, which stirs the beans while a powerful fan draws room-temperature air through the bean pile to cool it rapidly.

The best classic drum roasters have a *double drum* of two concentric layers of metal separated by a gap several millimeters wide. In a double drum, direct contact with the flame heats the outer drum, while the inner drum remains cooler. A double drum decreases conductive heat transfer and limits the risk of *tipping, scorching,* and *facing.* (Henceforth, these three are referred to in this text as "bean-surface burning.") If you buy a classic drum roaster, I strongly suggest finding one that has a double drum.

Advantages: The single pass of the roasting gas provides a clean roasting environment, and the drum serves as an effective heat-storage system, providing conductive heat transfer, especially during the first few minutes of a batch.

Disadvantage: Overheating the drum metal can easily lead to bean-surface burning.

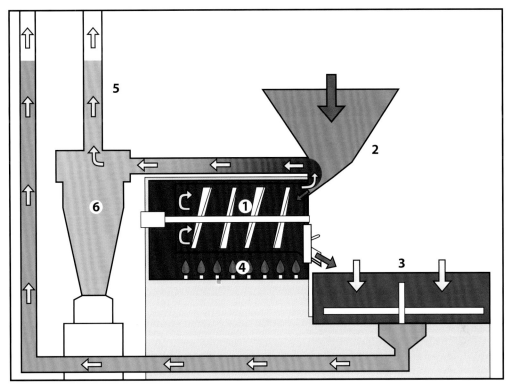

Classic drum roaster. Beans (brown arrows) enter the roasting drum (1) through the loading funnel (2). After roasting, the beans cool in the cooling bin (3). Air (blue arrows) passes from the combustion chamber (4) through the roasting drum and exhausts through the chimney (5) by way of the cyclone (6), which traps chaff.

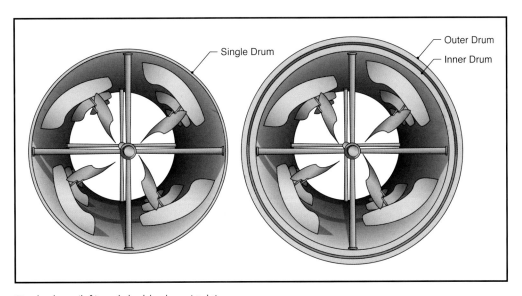

Single drum (left) and double drum (right)

Probat UG

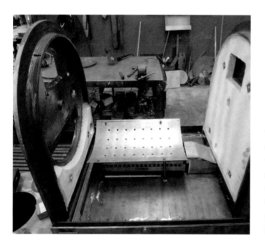

To decrease costs, some manufacturers have abandoned the double drum and substituted a static plate, or "heat shield," between the flame and drum. Despite these manufacturers' claims, single-layer drums with heat shields are usually inferior to double drums. The problem is that the heat shield gets extraordinarily hot because it is stationary and in constant contact with the flame. (A double drum's rotation prevents any one area from overheating due to continual contact with the flame.) I measured one heat shield at 950°F (510°C) with an infrared thermometer during a typical roast. The heat shield interferes with the machine operator's control of a roast by radiating large quantities of heat even when the flame is off.

Indirectly Heated Drum

Machines with indirectly heated drums send hot air from a combustion chamber through the roasting drum. This design protects the drum from direct flame contact, allowing the machine operator to use higher roasting temperatures with less risk of bean-surface burning. Like classic drum roasters, indirectly heated drum roasters mix the beans in the drum for even roasting and dump the beans into a separate cooling bin for efficient cooling at the end of a roast.

Advantages: Indirectly heated drums provide a clean roasting environment

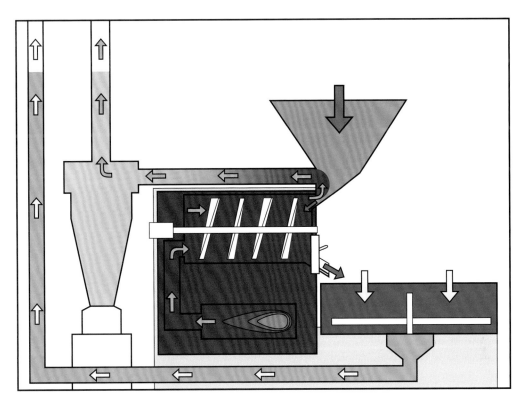

Indirectly heated drum roaster

This Joper has an indirectly heated drum.

and permit faster roasting at higher temperatures, with less risk of bean-surface burning, than most drum-roaster designs.

Disadvantage: This design is a little less fuel efficient than the classic drum roaster.

Fluid-Bed

Fluid-bed roasters rely on high airflow to keep the beans aloft and rotating in the roasting chamber. Because beans lose density as they roast, to maintain proper bean rotation these machines require very high airflow early in a roast and declining amounts of airflow as a batch progresses.[16]

Most fluid-bed roasters do not include a separate cooling bin; instead, room temperature air is passed through the roasting chamber at the end of a batch to cool the beans. This system is not ideal because the chamber's surfaces are hot, which inhibits the cooling process. Many users of fluid-bed roasters buy and use separate cooling bins.

Advantages: Fluid-bed roasters are affordable and reliable, have a small footprint, and pose little risk of bean-surface burning.

Disadvantages: Excessive airflow damages flavor and decreases fuel efficiency; the machine operator must compromise between the gas and airflow settings desired for optimal flavor and those required for proper bean rotation.

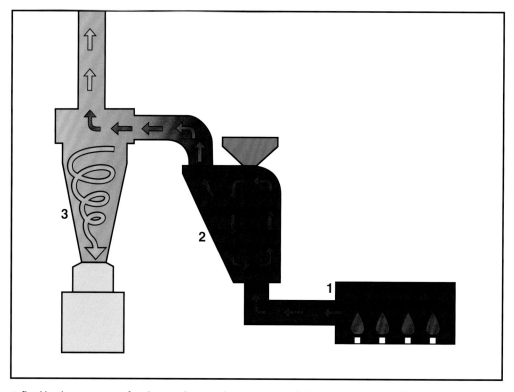

A fluid-bed roaster transfers heat to beans almost exclusively by convection. Air heated in the burner box (1) passes through the roasting chamber (2) and leaves the roaster through the chimney, while the cyclone (3) traps chaff. The beans enter the roaster through the funnel (green), circulate on a bed of hot air in the roasting chamber, and exit the roasting chamber through a door (not shown).

THE COFFEE ROASTER'S COMPANION

Recirculation

In contrast to the single-pass roasters listed above, recirculation roasters send a portion of a roast's exhaust air back through the burner chamber to recapture its heat, thereby decreasing the fuel requirements of the roasting process. These machines have recently become popular by virtue of being very

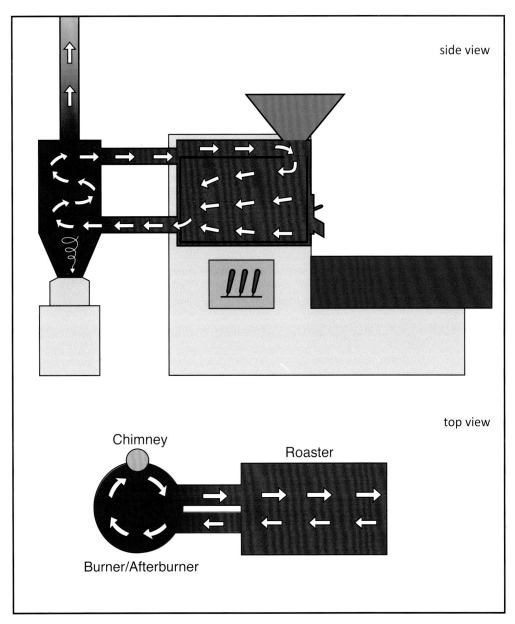

This recirculation roaster sends most of the exhaust air back through the drum and transfers heat almost exclusively by convection. In this design the burner also serves as the afterburner, incinerating particulate in the exhaust air before sending a portion of it up the chimney. The white arrows represent airflow. As in the drum-roaster illustration on page 23, beans enter the roaster through the green funnel, roast in the roasting drum (orange), and cool in the cooling bin (blue).

The Lilla (left) is an early attempt at a recirculating-air design, while the Loring is the best-in-class design.

fuel efficient, limiting bean-surface burning, and providing a very stable, moist, and repeatable roasting environment. The stable environment offers the side benefit of improving the ability of automated roasting software to track a programmed roast profile. The one significant drawback to these machines is a higher risk of smoky flavors in the coffee due to the beans dwelling in smokier air during roasting.

Advantages: Recirculation roasters offer fuel efficiency and fast roasting, with limited risk of bean-surface burning. They facilitate performance of automated profiling software, if any is used.

Disadvantage: Roasters sometimes report development of smoky flavors.

▪ 8 ▪

Progression
of a Roast

R oasters tend to focus most on the first and last stages of a roast batch, known respectively as the "drying phase" and "development time." While these terms have some validity, they're oversimplifications that can lead to misunderstanding of the roasting process. As we'll see, the entire roast curve influences drying and development during roasting.

The Illusion of the S Curve

Roast profile curves generally follow an "S" curve in which bean temperature drops precipitously for 70–90 seconds, bottoms out, and then rapidly increases. In reality, bean temperature does not drop: The beans enter the roaster at room

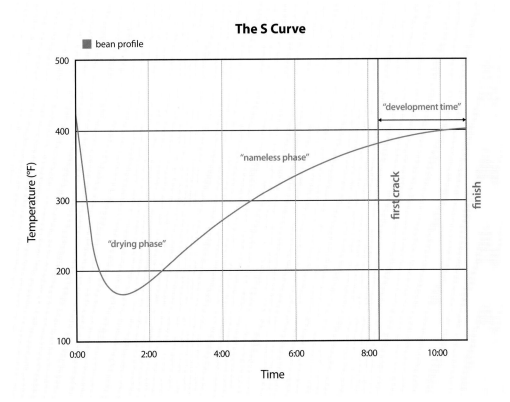

The S curve is the standard representation of bean-probe temperature readings during a roast. After bottoming at "the turn," the probe's readings increase rapidly at first and then at progressively slower rates throughout the remainder of a roast.

> I cannot overemphasize this fact: The bean-probe readout is merely a proxy for the surface temperatures of the bean pile. It does not perfectly represent the surface temperatures of the beans. It's not necessarily that the probe is inaccurate; the probe is merely doing its job of reading the temperature of the media in which it is immersed. In the case of coffee roasting, that medium is a combination of beans and hot gases.

temperature and immediately get hotter. The apparent initial temperature decrease is an artifact of the air in the roaster influencing the bean probe, as well as the probe's *thermometric lag.* I recommend not getting too hung up on the first 2–3 minutes' worth of bean-probe readings; in most roasting machines the bean probe becomes a useful guide sometime during the third minute.

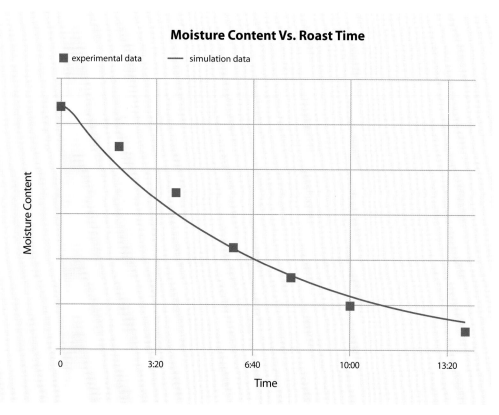

As the graphic above shows, beans lose moisture at a steady rate until first crack. (Adapted with gracious permission from: Bottazzi, D.; Farina, S.; Milani, M.; Montorsi, M. (2012) A numerical approach for the analysis of the coffee roasting process. *Journal of Food Engineering.* 112, 243–252. Original data compiled by: Schenker, S. (2000) Investigations on the hot air roasting of coffee beans. Swiss Federal Institute of Technology, Zurich.)

The Myth of the Drying Phase

One of my personal peeves when discussing roasting is the use of the misleading terms "drying phase" and "development time." Roasting is a complex process in which development and moisture loss, among other changes, occur continuously throughout a batch. The practice of referring to the first phase of roasting as the "drying phase" and the last stage as "development time" has led to much misunderstanding of the roasting process.

The Middle (Nameless) Phase

At a few minutes into a roast, once the beans have turned a shade of tan or light brown, begins the neglected, nameless, middle phase. During this phase sugars break down to form acids[19] and the beans release steam, begin to expand, and emit pleasant, bready aromas. The changes in color and aroma are largely the work of Maillard reactions, which accelerate as bean temperatures reach approximately 250°F–300°F (121°C–149°C).

At approximately 340°F (171°C), caramelization begins, which degrades sugars, thus slowing the Maillard reactions by stealing their fuel. Caramelization deepens the beans' brown color and creates fruity, caramelly, and nutty aromas. Both Maillard reactions and caramelization decrease coffee's sweetness and increase bitterness.

During this (nameless) phase, expansion of the beans causes them to shed their chaff, or silver skin. Simultaneously, smoke develops, and the machine operator must ensure the airflow is high enough to exhaust the chaff and smoke as it forms. Inadequate airflow at this stage may lead to smoky-flavored coffee and could create a fire hazard if chaff builds up excessively in certain areas of the roaster.

First Crack

While the process of roasting beans can be monotonous at times, first crack is always exciting. The bean pile emits a series of popping noises that begins quietly, accelerates, reaches a crescendo, and then tapers. The beans spontaneously expand and expel chaff, and smoke development intensifies. As noted earlier, first crack represents the audible release of pent-up water vapor and CO_2 pressure from the bean core.

According to Illy[5] and Eggers,[30] bean surface temperatures decrease for a brief period (probably several seconds, though your bean probe will likely not indicate this change), a phenomenon known as the *endothermic flash*. The flash is due to the surface-cooling effect of evaporation as large amounts of water vapor escape the beans.

Shortly before first crack, the bean-pile temperature's *rate of rise* (ROR) is prone to level off. It tends to plummet at around the time of the endothermic flash and will often accelerate rapidly after the flash. These shifts in the ROR are undesirable, and I discuss them in depth later in this book. (See "The Bean Temperature Progression Shalt Always Decelerate" in Chapter 10.)

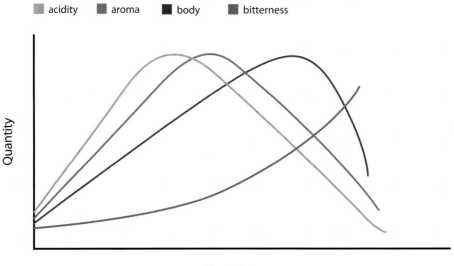

Evolution of Cup Quality During Roasting

■ acidity ■ aroma ■ body ■ bitterness

Quantity (vertical axis) · *Roast Degree* (horizontal axis)

Acidity increases during roasting until the beans reach a city roast and declines with further roasting. Aromatics peak shortly afterward, in the range of city to full city roast. Body increases until a roast reaches a very dark color somewhere in the vicinity of French roast, after which body declines. Extraction potential is maximized at a French roast and decreases thereafter as pyrolysis burns off soluble mass.

Second Crack

After the completion of first crack there is a quiet lull during which CO_2 pressure builds anew in the bean core. The pressure is able to force oils to the bean surface because pyrolysis and the trauma of first crack have weakened the bean's cellulose structure. Right around the time the first beads of oil appear on bean surfaces, second crack begins, releasing CO_2 pressure and oils from the inner bean.

Roasting into second crack destroys much of a coffee's unique character because caramelization and pyrolysis yield heavy, pungent, and roasty flavors that overwhelm whatever subtle flavors survive such dark roasting. In the cup, dark roasts exhibit bittersweet and smoky flavors; heavy, syrupy body; and minimal acidity. If roasting is taken much further than early second crack, then burnt, carbonized flavors appear and body declines. While perhaps the majority of specialty coffee chains roast into second crack, today's progressive specialty roasters rarely do.

Development Time

Many roasters refer to the time from the onset of first crack until discharging the beans as "development time." This is a misleading term that oversimplifies the roasting process. As shown in the graph "Inner Vs. Outer Bean Temperature," on page 20, after the first several seconds a batch is in the roaster, inner-bean development occurs continually until the end of the roast. Roasters often attempt to improve development, especially in roasts for espresso, by lengthening the roast time after first crack. Extending the roast time after first crack will usually increase development of the bean core, but the more efficient way to improve inner-bean development is to create a larger temperature gradient earlier in the roast. Intentionally extending the last few minutes of a roast usually creates *baked* flavors and should be avoided.

> It is vital to understand that the shape of the entire roast curve influences bean development.

It is vital to understand that the shape of the entire roast curve influences bean development and moisture loss. In Chapter 10, "The Three Commandments of Roasting," I discuss how to shape the roast curve to enhance bean development and sweetness while eliminating the risk of creating baked flavors.

▪ 9 ▪
Planning a Roast Batch

A roaster must make many decisions before charging a batch of coffee. He must consider batch size, machine design, and various bean characteristics before choosing the charge temperature, initial gas setting, and airflow.

Batch Size

The first step when planning a roast is to determine a machine's optimal range of batch sizes. One must consider a machine's drum size, airflow range, and rated burner output to decide what batch sizes will taste best. One should not assume that a roaster's stated capacity is its optimal batch size; I have found that many, if not most, machines produce the best coffee at 50%–70% of their nominal capacity.

Roasting machine manufacturers are motivated to exaggerate their machines' capacities because most buyers, especially of small, specialty machines, are influenced by that headline number.* One can estimate a machine's realistic maximum batch size by first noting the machine's stated capacity. That number most likely represents the largest batch a roaster should attempt to put into that machine's drum. Filling a drum past its stated capacity may lead to less effective mixing of beans during roasting or to the exhaust fan sucking beans out of the roaster.

> Most single-pass drum roasters can effectively roast 1 lb of coffee per 5000 BTU (i.e., 1 kg per 11,606 kJ) of rated power output.

The next, and usually most important, consideration is a machine's stated power output. Researchers estimate that 1 kg of 20°C green coffee requires 1000–1500 kJ (948–1422 BTU) to reach a medium roast.[5, 32] However, the typical single-pass roaster is inefficient, transferring only a portion of its burner energy to the beans. Much of its heat is lost up the stack, and some is lost to the roasting room and other areas. My experience with dozens of different machines indicates that real-world, single-pass roasting is 50%–75% efficient. In other words, single-pass roasters consume up to twice as much energy than they transfer to the beans.

Therefore, if your 12 kg machine has a rating of 100,000 BTU (105,506 kJ),

---

* This problem is akin to that in the marketing of home coffee brewers: Today's "12-cup" brewer typically brews a mere 50–60 oz of coffee. Over the years, the definition of a cup's volume has shrunk to 4 oz or 5 oz, apparently subject to the whims of the manufacturer's marketing department.

your maximum batch should be approximately 20 lb (9 kg). With some experimentation, you may find that your preferred batch size is a little larger or smaller, and it will vary with different beans, but I recommend a batch size of 20 lb (9 kg) as the starting point for experimentation. Fluid-bed roasters are less efficient than single-pass drum roasters, and recirculation roasters are more efficient than single-pass machines, so they can accommodate different batch sizes relative to their burner ratings. The efficiency of a recirculation roaster increases with the proportion of heat it recycles.

Most machines have no minimum batch size, assuming they are capable of idling with constant gas settings at temperatures as low as 400°F (204°C). However, several practical considerations make roasting very small batches (those smaller than 25% of a machine's capacity) challenging.

Among other considerations, very small batches require

- Less airflow. Too much airflow may suck beans out of the roaster, especially if the drum's revolutions per minute (RPM) rate is too high.
- Slower drum speeds. At standard drum RPM, the beans may ricochet around the roasting drum, which can cause uneven roasting and loss of beans into the exhaust airstream.
- A machine operator willing and able to roast without using a bean probe. When a batch is so small that the probe is not immersed in the bean pile, the probe becomes less reliable, or even useless.*

Setting Airflow

For years I've been adjusting airflow settings based on a simple test using a cigarette lighter. To perform the test, remove the trowel from the machine while a batch is roasting and the gas is on. Hold a lit cigarette lighter up the trowel hole and note whether the flame leans toward the hole, away from the hole, or remains vertical. Adjust the airflow such that the flame leans gently toward the hole, indicating a slight draw. (Increasing the airflow will pull the flame more strongly.) If the flame does not lean toward the hole, there is insufficient draw to adequately exhaust the waste products of combustion and roasting. A flame pulling strongly toward the hole, or extinguished by the airflow into the hole, indicates too much draw.

A similar test may be done by holding a small, thin piece of paper, larger than the trowel hole, up to the hole. A reasonable airflow setting should provide just enough draw to hold the paper against the hole so that it won't fall if you let go.

Coffee roasting requires less airflow earlier in a roast and more airflow later. Once the beans begin to emit smoke and shed chaff, more airflow becomes necessary. Increasing the airflow during a roast increases convective heat transfer, so, if possible, increase airflow gradually and incrementally. A large one-time increase in airflow may interfere with the smooth deceleration

---

* I successfully roasted twenty 100-g samples from the 2006 "Best of Panama" auction in a 23-kg Gothot machine by ignoring the bean probe and focusing on other parameters, such as replicating a particular air-temperature profile each batch.

of the bean-temperature progression. (See "The Bean Temperature Progression Shalt Always Decelerate" in Chapter 10.)

Some roasting machines with fuel injectors, or "power burners," require the airflow and gas settings to increase and decrease in tandem to maintain a constant air–fuel ratio for efficient combustion. This presents a conundrum for the machine operator, since ideal roasting calls for gas settings to begin high and remain steady or decrease throughout a batch and for airflow to be relatively high later in a batch. There is no wide-ranging solution to this problem with power-burner machines, as they're all different, and roasters must address this situation on a case-by-case basis.

Plan a roast's airflow settings ahead of time, knowing what the initial airflow will be, when the roast's airflow will change, and by how much. Between batches, low-to-moderate airflow is appropriate, as it allows the operator to maintain a steady environmental temperature without using an unnecessarily large flame.

Adjusting the Air–Fuel Ratio

If your burner system allows, adjust the flame so that it appears blue with orange streaks (the orange color is caused by dust in the air). If your flame is lazy and yellow, it indicates a lack of air and incomplete combustion.[1] A flame starved of air will produce more soot, smoke, and carbon monoxide, and less carbon dioxide, than it should. If your flame lifts off the burner and sounds a bit like a blowtorch, it is getting too much air.[1] (Ideally, allow the roaster to equilibrate for a few minutes before judging whether the mixture needs adjustment.)

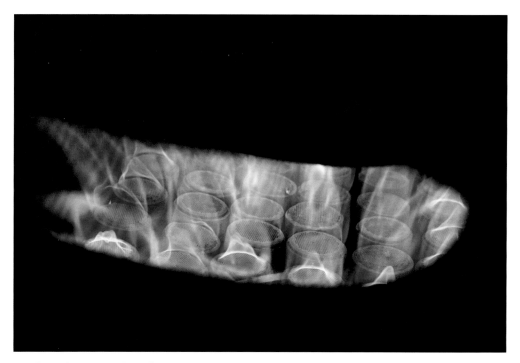

This flame has an ideal air–fuel ratio.

The ideal air–fuel ratio is approximately 10:1, though it is customary to set it a little higher as a buffer against changes in air temperature or moisture.[12]

Charge Temperature

The charge temperature* and initial gas setting of a batch are critical determinants of the course of a roast profile. Charging at too low a temperature can limit bean development or force the use of an excessive initial gas setting, causing the drum to overheat. Charging too hot can burn a bean or blunt some of the delicacy of its potential flavor. Knowing how to balance charge temperature and initial gas setting, as well as how to manage a roaster before charging, are essential to ensuring that every batch follows an optimal profile. To determine the charge temperature, one must consider roasting-machine design, batch size, bean density, bean size, bean-processing method, and intended roast time.

Machine Design

The first step in choosing a charge temperature is to consider the type of roasting machine one is using. A machine with direct contact between the flame and drum has a hotter drum, relative to the roasting environment, than does a machine that heats the drum indirectly. One must limit charge temperatures when using directly heated drums because such drums pose greater risk of scorching the beans.

Fluid-bed roasters, lacking drums and conductive heat transfer, can accommodate the hottest charges, at well over 550°F (288°C). Indirectly heated drum machines and machines with perforated drums can handle hot charges in the range of 450°F–525°F (232°C–274°C). Classic drum roasters require varying degrees of caution, depending on the thickness and material of the drum and whether it is single- or double-walled. Reasonable charge temperatures range from 380°F–440°F (193°C–227°C).**

---

* "Charge temperature" is a slippery concept. While it always refers to the empty roaster's air temperature just before beans are loaded into the machine, there is no consensus on what temperature one is referring to: Some machine operators base charge temperature on the bean probe reading, others base it on the air probe reading. Those two readings are not only non-transferable between machines, but two consecutive identical batches charged in the same machine at a probe reading of, for example, 400°F (204°C) may behave quite differently. The problem is that charge temperature is an incomplete, and often inconsistent, representation of a machine's thermal energy. For example, in the scenario above, the machine's drum surface temperature may have been 500°F (260°C) when charging the first batch but 520°F (271°C) during the second batch's charge. That small difference in drum temperature will result in different roast profiles. All operators have experienced this phenomenon when trying to make the first batch of a roast day behave identically to batches roasted later in that session. Most operators just accept that their first two or three batches each day will roast differently from later batches, and they try to work around the problem by roasting decaf or particularly small batches first, each session. In "Between-Batch Protocol" in Chapter 11, I discuss how to reset a machine's thermal energy before each batch to ensure consistent results, even on the first batch of the day.

**These numbers refer to bean-probe temperatures after 1–2 minutes of idling between batches.

As noted earlier, the drum in a classic drum roaster acts as a heat-storage device, storing tens of thousands of kilojoules of heat energy. This stored energy contributes to heat transfer early in a roast and compensates for some or all of the lower charge temperatures that directly heated drums demand. Adequate heat transfer during the first minutes of a roast is critical to inner-bean development. (See "Thou Shalt Apply Adequate Energy at the Beginning of a Roast" in Chapter 10.)

Batch Size

The larger the batch, the greater the drop in a roaster's environmental temperature upon charging. Therefore, larger batches require hotter charge temperatures to ensure sufficient heat transfer during the first minute or two of a roast.

Bean Density

For a given bean size, it requires more energy to penetrate the core of denser beans. Charging hotter is often appropriate for exceptionally dense beans.

Bean Size

Because a larger bean has more distance from its surface to its core, penetrating a larger bean requires more energy.

Bean Processing Method

The processing of green coffee affects its density, its susceptibility to burning, and, often, its moisture content. When planning a roast, one must consider green processing on a case-by-case basis due to the myriad variables it involves. As a rule, washed-process coffees require, and can tolerate, hotter charging temperatures than natural-process ones can.

Intended Roast Time

Charge temperature and roast time must be considered together. All else being equal, one should charge hotter when roasting faster. A faster roast calls for establishing a larger ΔT early in the batch to ensure sufficient development. Insufficient charge temperature will impede inner-bean development. Likewise, slower roasts call for cooler charges. Charging a long roast at too hot a setting will force the machine operator to slow the roast excessively, at some point, in order to extend the total roast time. Such deceleration may create baked flavors or inhibit development.

One must consider all six of the preceding variables (machine design, batch size, bean density, bean size, bean processing method, and intended roast time) when deciding an appropriate charge temperature for a batch. For example, in a 30 kg–capacity classic drum roaster, one may charge a 12-minute, 25 kg batch of large, dense, washed Kenya AA beans at 430°F (221°C). In the same machine, the roaster may choose a 380°F (193°C) charge for a 15-minute, 20 kg batch of a small, low-density, naturally processed Brazilian. (Please ignore the unusual choice to roast the larger batch of Kenya so much faster than the Brazilian.)

In these examples, the classic drum roaster calls for a modest charge temperature for both batches. The Kenya's larger batch and bean sizes, greater density, and washed processing each contribute to its need for a hotter charge than the Brazilian requires. Please note that these examples are hypothetical, and your beans and machine may require radically different temperatures.

Determining Roast Time

The roasting industry harbors a nearly universal misconception that slower roasting yields better development. While it's true that roasting too fast will produce *underdeveloped* coffee, roasting slowly will not necessarily ensure good development. It is neither total roast time nor "development time" that determines final development. The shape of the entire roast curve influences development.

Assuming the size of a roast batch is less than or equal to a machine's realistic capacity (see "Batch Size" in Chapter 9), a wide range of roast curves and times can create coffee with good development and flavor. I cannot tell you the exact, optimal time range for roasts in your machine, but I offer the following suggestions as rough estimates.

Recommended Roast Time Ranges	
Machine Type	**Minutes:Seconds**
Classic drum roasters	10:00–16:00
Indirectly heated drum roasters and roasters with perforated drums	9:00–15:00
Fluid-bed roasters	7:00–11:00

For any given machine, smaller batches require less time to achieve adequate development. Bean density, bean size, green-coffee moisture content, and roast degree may also affect optimal roast time.

Drum RPM

One should set the revolutions per minute (RPM) of the roasting drum's rotation primarily based on the drum's inner diameter and the size of a roast batch. The RPM setting should provide optimal mixing of the beans to create an even roast while minimizing the risk of bean-surface burning. Based on my experience and an informal survey of several roasting companies, I recommend the following guidelines for drum RPM when roasting batches of 60%–80% of stated capacity.

Suggested Drum RPM	
Stated Roaster Capacity	**RPM**
5–12 kg	52–54 RPM
15–22 kg	50–52 RPM
30–45 kg	48–50 RPM

These numbers are meant as rough guides based on typical drum dimensions. The true evidence of appropriate drum RPM is the uniform mixing and roasting of the beans and the minimization of bean-surface burning.

Roasters should consider the following factors when setting drum RPM:

• Higher drum RPM slightly increases airflow and convective heat transfer.
• Smaller batches call for lower drum RPM.

- If your machine's drum speed is easy to adjust, consider gradually increasing the rotation by a few RPM as a batch progresses. This will maintain even mixing and rotation of the beans as they expand. (Think of the expansion of the beans as akin to an increase in batch size.)

Bean Moisture, Density, and Size

Most roasters seem to use trial and error to figure out how to roast each new lot of green coffee. The process may range in length from a few days to a few weeks before the roaster settles on roast settings for the new coffee. Meanwhile, the roaster's customers receive inconsistent and often subpar roasts during the experimentation process.

While any new lot may require some special treatment, roasters can bypass most of the trial and error by measuring every green coffee's density, bean size, and moisture content. Knowing those three measurements allows a roaster to predict how to apply heat to the beans during roasting. The details of how to translate the measurements into roasting decisions are beyond the scope of this book, but I recommend tracking these three data points (density, bean size, and moisture content) for every lot of green coffee and noticing the relationships between those measurements and the roasting results.

■ 10 ■

The Three Commandments of Roasting

Please don't take the word "commandment" too seriously. One may transgress some of these rules harmlessly on occasion. As with a certain other list of commandments, however, if you make a habit of ignoring the rules, you might end up in a bad place.

As a roaster and a consultant over the past nineteen years, I've had the opportunity to cup and view the roast data for each of more than 20,000 batches roasted on a variety of machines by various methods. About five years ago, I spent several days poring over reams of roast data in an attempt to find the common elements in the best batches I'd ever tasted.* To be clear, I'm not referring to "really good" batches. I focused only on the data from batches so special that I could "taste" them in my memory months or years after physically tasting them. That effort yielded what I think of as the "commandments of roasting."

A method graduated to a commandment only if it seemed to apply to a great variety of coffees and roasting machines. I've been testing and refining the commandments for five years, and so far I've yet to find a situation in which coffee tastes better when a commandment is broken. I've also had opportunities to test the commandments in reverse; the times I've tasted stellar roasts from others and the roaster was kind enough to share the roast data with me, sure enough, the profiles conformed to the commandments.

I can't fully explain why these methods work. But I'm confident that if you remain open-minded and apply these techniques carefully and completely, you will be impressed by how much better your roasts taste.

I. Thou Shalt Apply Adequate Energy at the Beginning of a Roast

Applying sufficient heat at the beginning of a roast is essential to achieving optimal flavor and proper bean development. While one may begin a roast with too little heat and still cook the bean centers adequately, the flavor of such coffee may suffer because the operator must lengthen the roast time excessively to compensate for the insufficient early heat transfer.

---

* I compiled and evaluated my roast data by using a pencil, calculator, and spreadsheet. These days one can analyze such data much more efficiently with the aid of computer software such as Cropster's "Roast Ranger" application.

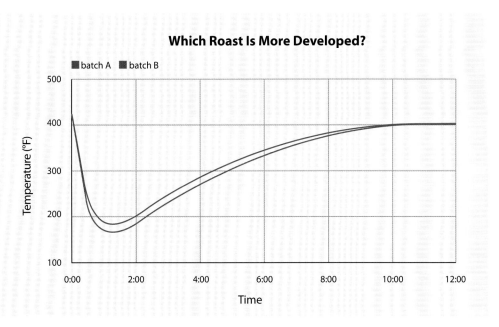

Which Roast Is More Developed?

Batch A and batch B had identical charge temperature, drop temperature, and roast time. Given that batch A's bean temperature initially rose more quickly than batch B's, batch A is more developed.

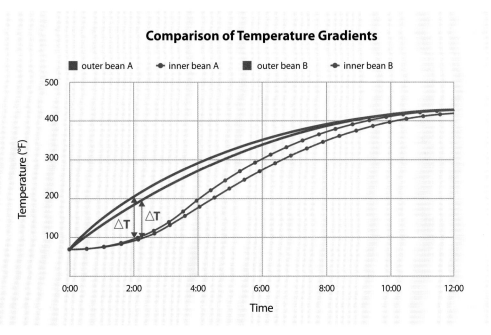

Comparison of Temperature Gradients

This graph illustrates the importance of establishing a large ΔT early in a roast. In batch A, the machine operator applied sufficient energy early in the roast, creating a large ΔT, which gave the inner bean the impetus to smoothly "catch up" to the outer bean by the end of the roast. Batch B began sluggishly, creating a smaller early ΔT. Relative to batch A, the operator applied more heat mid-roast to adequately cook the outer bean in a similar total roast time. However, the extra energy was too little, too late for the inner bean's temperature to match that of the outer bean, and batch B was underdeveloped.

II. The Bean Temperature Progression Shalt Always Decelerate

In every batch, the bean-temperature's rate of rise (ROR) initially increases at a rapid rate and then decreases as the coffee roasts. That's the natural result of putting room-temperature beans into a hot roaster. The machine operator's goal should be to produce an always-declining ROR. Should the ROR increase during a roast (other than the illusory increase in ROR during the first 2–3 minutes of a roast), development will suffer and some of the coffee's potential sweetness will be sacrificed.

If the ROR is constant or horizontal, even for just 1 minute, it will also destroy sweetness and create "flat" flavors reminiscent of paper, cardboard, dry cereal, or straw. Every time I've tasted this flaw in a coffee and had the opportunity to view its roast data, the ROR had flatlined.

If the ROR declines at a moderate, steady pace and then drops precipitously, it compromises development, and unless the roast is discharged immediately, baked flavors develop. Baked flavors are similar to, but more extreme than, the flat, dull flavors created by a constant ROR. Should a roast stall, meaning the bean temperature stops rising (i.e., the ROR is 0 or has a negative value), baked flavors will dominate and sweetness will all but disappear. Researchers have not, to my knowledge, established the chemistry of baked coffee flavors.

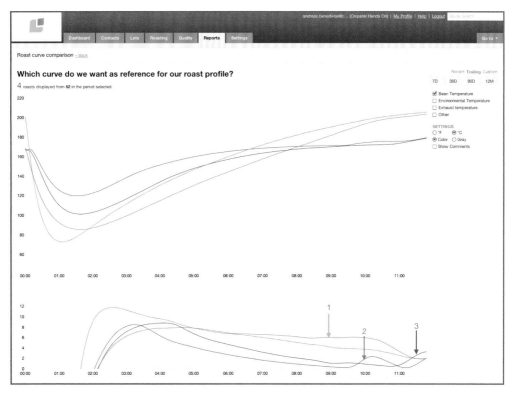

The top graph shows four roast profiles and the bottom graph illustrates their respective ROR curves. The long, flat section (1) of the green ROR curve indicates the coffee will taste flat and lack sweetness. The increases, or "flicks," (2 and 3) in the blue and red ROR curves indicate those roasts did not develop as much as they could have at their respective roast degrees. The yellow profile and its corresponding ROR curve have no obvious problems. (Graphs graciously provided by Cropster.)

The leading theory is that a stall in a roast causes developing sugar chains to "cross-link," which decreases sweetness and creates baked flavors.

For clarification, the following profiles illustrate various ROR patterns.

Experienced roasters know the ROR has a natural tendency to change course at particular moments. Perhaps the most challenging stretch of a roast occurs during first crack. To achieve a smoothly decreasing ROR, the operator must anticipate and adjust for each of the following common situations:

- The ROR often flatlines at some point during the minute or two before first crack.
- The ROR tends to drop sharply during first crack due to evaporative cooling.
- After first crack, the ROR tends to turn upward rapidly.*
- At or after second crack, the ROR reaccelerates.

A Typical Roast Profile and Its ROR Curve

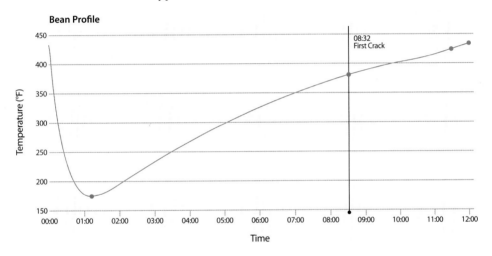

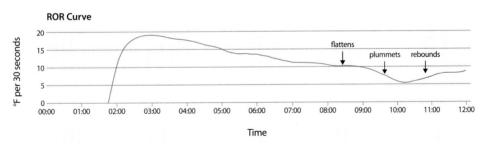

A typical roast curve's profile and ROR at around first crack, adapted from a Cropster-generated screenshot. An ROR curve often flattens before first crack, plummets as evaporation peaks, and rebounds as first crack ends. Most roasters are so used to this pattern that they are not aware it damages coffee flavor.

---

* The ROR's tendency to accelerate around both cracks presumably indicates two *exothermic* phases.

III. First Crack Shalt Begin at 75% to 80% of Total Roast Time

Experience has taught me that the roast time from the onset of first crack* to the end of a roast should make up 20%–25% of total roast time. Put another way, the "development-time ratio" (DTR) should be between 20%–25% of total roast time. I'm confident that the optimal ratio is actually in a much narrower range, and the ratio should vary slightly depending on roast degree desired, but I don't have enough data yet to back up those beliefs.

If the DTR is greater than 20%–25% of total roast time, the coffee will probably taste flat. If the DTR is less than 20%–25% of total roast time, development will likely be insufficient.

Most roasters seem to adjust a roast's development time separately from the rest of the roast curve, but such an approach will often lead to baked flavors or underdevelopment. Instead of focusing on development time, I recommend that roasters adjust the last phase of a roast curve to ensure it is proportional to the entire roast curve. I hope roasters will find this suggested ratio useful and that the conversation among roasters shifts from "development time" to "development time ratio" or a similar phrase.

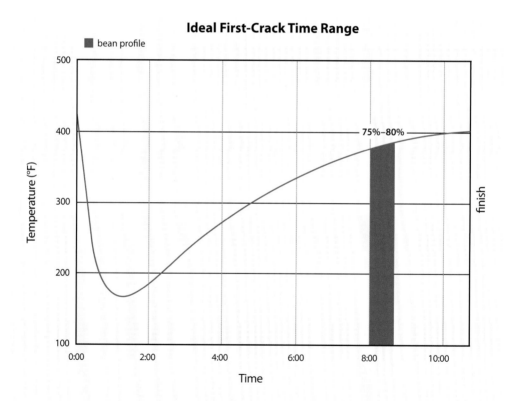

First crack should ideally begin in the shaded zone.

---

* I consider the beginning of first crack to be the moment the operator hears more than one or two isolated pops.

Applying the Commandments to Very Light Roasting

As stated in the Introduction, my recommendations apply to "light-to-medium roasts." By that, I mean roasts dropped after the completion of first crack, but before the onset of second crack. I have found that proper application of the recommendations for such roast levels has always improved results.

There is one special situation that merits mention: very light, Nordic-style roasting. Since the publication of the first edition of this book, many roasters have inquired about the appropriateness of a 20%–25% development time ratio for very light roasts (ie those dropped midway through first crack.) While the best roasts I've ever tasted all had DTRs greater than 20%, I wouldn't neces- sarily recommend such high DTRs for roasts dropped during first crack. For example, if one were to drop a batch a few seconds after first crack began, it would be impractical to aim for a 20% DTR.

I can't prescribe an ideal DTR range for such light roasts. Both the lightness of the roast and the amount of momentum the roast has upon hitting first crack

First crack is like breaking a sweat.

Imagine you are running outside on a hot day. Normally, your body sweats a little each second to lower your body temperature and prevent overheat- ing, a process known as "evaporative cooling." Let's pretend that your body "forgets" to sweat for 5 minutes, and that at the end of that 5 minutes, your body releases all of the sweat it forgot to produce. In this unrealistic scenario, your body temperature would rise for 5 minutes and then rapidly cool, perhaps so much so that your skin would briefly feel cold.

A well-functioning body, sweating at a steady rate, is the equivalent of a smoothly declining ROR. On the other hand, the forgetful body that over- heats and then rapidly cools is like the typical ROR curve that levels off or rises just before first crack, and then crashes after first crack begins.

First crack represents a release of moisture analogous to a human sweat- ing. In the case of coffee roasting, it's intuitively appealing to have all of the beans crack at the same moment, as that would imply the beans were all roasting at the same rate. However, in a roasting machine full of beans, if too many beans crack at the same time, their cumulative moisture release would cool the roasting system too much (resulting in the ROR crash) and slow or stall the roast.

If one intends to roast beyond the end of first crack, I recommend maintain- ing a steadily declining ROR to prevent a strong crack that cools the roast- ing environment too rapidly. However, if a roaster plans to end a batch during first crack, it may be wise to enter first crack with more momentum, to attempt to make the beans crack almost simultaneously, and drop the batch before the roasting environment cools too much.

will influence the appropriate DTR. (Think of a roast's momentum in the final seconds as an extension of development time.) I recommend, however, that the lighter one roasts, and the lower the DTR is at the end of a roast, the higher the ROR should be as first crack begins.

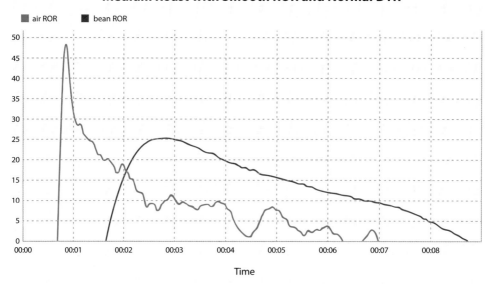

A medium roast with a smooth ROR and 20% DTR

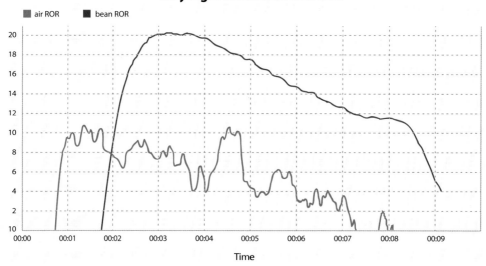

A very light roast with high ROR entering first crack and low DTR

· 11 ·

Mastering Consistency

Much like the elusive "God shot" of espresso, most companies roast the occasional great batch but can't seem to reproduce it consistently. Variations in a roaster's thermal energy, green-coffee temperature and moisture, ambient conditions, and chimney cleanliness all collude to make roasting inconsistent. I've designed the tips in this chapter to help you control or lessen the impacts of these factors. Following these recommendations will help any roaster improve consistency.

How to Warm Up a Roaster

At a cupping of some lovely Cup of Excellence coffees a few years ago, I noticed that one of the samples was very underdeveloped and another was slightly underdeveloped. The other cups had varying degrees of good development. It dawned on me that those two cups had been brewed from, respectively, the first and second batches roasted that day. I suggested to my cupping host the order in which he had roasted the samples that morning. I had guessed the order correctly.

Every roaster I've ever asked has admitted to having difficulty with the quality of the first few batches of a roasting session. The problem is usually caused by inadequate warming up of the roasting machine. Most machine operators warm up a roaster to the charge temperature and then idle the machine at or near that temperature for some amount of time, usually 15–30 minutes, before charging the first batch. This protocol guarantees that the first batch will roast sluggishly compared with successive batches.

The problem is that temperature probes are poor indicators of a machine's thermal energy. (See "Charge Temperature" in Chapter 9.) As a cold roasting machine warms up, although the temperature probes quickly indicate that the air in the machine has reached roasting-level temperatures, the mass of the machine is still much cooler than the air in the drum. If one charges a batch at this point, the machine's mass will behave akin to a *heat sink* and absorb heat from the roasting process, decreasing the rate of heat transfer to the beans. After several roast batches, the machine's thermal energy will reach an equilibrium range within which it will fluctuate for the remainder of the roasting session.

The trick to normalizing the results of the first few batches of a roasting session is to seemingly overheat the machine during the warm-up, before stabilizing it at normal roasting temperatures. To my knowledge, there is no practical, precise way to measure a roaster's thermal energy. However, the operator can apply some informed experimentation to establish a protocol that brings a roaster's thermal energy into its equilibrium range. The operator should employ this protocol prior to charging the first batch of every session.

I recommend the following procedure to determine an effective warm-up protocol for your roaster:

1. Set the airflow to the average level you will use during your roasts.
2. Using a medium-to-high gas setting, warm up the machine until the bean probe indicates 50°F (28°C) above your intended charge temperature.
3. Idle the machine at that temperature for 20 minutes.
4. Lower the gas setting so the temperature drops gradually.
5. Once the probe displays the charge temperature, idle the machine at that temperature for 10 minutes.
6. Charge the first batch.
7. Roast the first batch, using the same gas and airflow settings you would for a batch later in the day.
8. Compare this batch to the results you would typically get later in a roast session. If this batch roasted faster than desired, lower the peak warm-up temperature next time. If this batch was slow, idle at the peak warm-up temperature for a longer time.
9. Repeat step 8 each day, until your first batch behaves exactly as batches later in a roast session do.

Between-Batch Protocol

As important as the initial warm-up protocol is your between-batch protocol. One should follow an identical procedure after every batch to "reset" the roaster's thermal energy at the desired level before charging the next batch.

I suggest the following as an effective template for a between-batch protocol. Feel free to adjust this procedure to meet your machine's particular needs. I strongly suggest using a timer to ensure you make each adjustment at the same time, every time.

1. Decrease the airflow to the lowest level you will use during a roast batch.
2. Turn off the gas for 1 minute after dropping a roast batch. Adjust the gas to a setting that will bring the temperature probe to the intended charge temperature in 60–90 seconds.
3. Once the charge temperature is reached, idle there for 1 minute.
4. Charge the next batch.

The protocols for the initial warm-up and between batches are meant as guidelines to help one approach these transitions systematically. The operator will undoubtedly need to customize these protocols to achieve perfectly consistent batches. With some experimentation, these protocols should allow anyone to produce roasts that track their intended profiles almost identically every batch, with total roast times varying by no more than 5–10 seconds per batch.

Other Tips to Improve Batch-to-Batch Consistency

Several factors can complicate one's efforts to reset a roaster's thermal energy before charging a batch. These include variations in the size, environmental temperature, and roast degree of the previous batch. Therefore, there is a bit of an art to resetting the thermal energy, but one can employ a few strategies to improve the odds of success:

- Roast only one batch size. If that is not possible, roast all batches of a given size consecutively before roasting batches of a different size.
- Roast smaller batches first, then successively larger batches.
- Adjust the between-batch protocol after roasting unusually dark or light batches or batches ending at an exceptionally high or low environmental temperature. The machine will be hotter after dropping darker batches and batches roasted at higher temperatures. One may, for instance, turn the gas off for longer intervals after roasting darker batches.

Green-Coffee Storage and Consistency

I doubt that anyone would argue the fact that storing green coffee at consistent temperature and humidity is a good practice. While it's true that one may roast great coffee despite inconsistent green-storage conditions, proper storage makes consistent roasting results much more likely. I recommend storing your entire raw-coffee inventory in a climate-controlled environment, if possible. If that's too difficult or costly, consider at least using a "staging room." You can build such a room cheaply, furnish it with a thermostatically controlled space heater, and store in it only the green coffee to be roasted in the next week. For green coffee beans stored in hermetically sealed bags (vacuum-sealed or Grain-Pro), temperature control is all that is needed. Raw coffee exposed to the surrounding air, such as that stored in burlap, calls for control of both temperature and humidity. If you humidify your long-term green storage, you must monitor for mold and may have to rotate the placement of the bags in their piles to prevent mold growth.

Ambient Conditions

Variations in the atmosphere inside and outside the roastery are a fact of life. Other than attempting to control the climate of the roasting room as well as one can, my best advice is to focus on the bean-temperature profile when roasting and to adapt to changing conditions as necessary to maintain that profile. Colder and drier weather outside the roastery will increase draw in the stack due to *stack effect,* potentially increasing airflow in the roaster, and may necessitate adjustments to the roaster's exhaust fan or damper to maintain consistent airflow. Colder air in the roastery will alter the fuel mixture feeding the flame (the incoming air will be colder and hold more oxygen per unit of volume) and will require the operator to make adjustments to maintain the intended heat transfer.

Chimney Cleaning

Roasting deposits *creosote,* coffee oils, and various solid waste products of combustion and roasting on the inner walls of a roaster's exhaust ductwork. As these solids build up in the ducts they create friction and decrease airflow. Frequent scrubbing of the exhaust ducts is critical for maintaining consistent airflow and decreasing the risk of chimney fires.

Cleaning should be done on a schedule based on roasting volume and how dark one roasts. Darker roasting will require much more frequent chimney cleaning than lighter roasting. I hesitate to prescribe a particular schedule, given the variables involved, but recommend you clean your chimney at least every couple of hundred hours of roasting. If one uses an *afterburner,* the ducts downstream of the afterburner should rarely require cleaning.

Managing Different Batch Sizes

Roasting various batch sizes in a machine is not too difficult if the operator understands how to adjust several roast variables. Most importantly, for batches below a certain size, the bean probe will not be fully immersed in the bean pile and will read less accurately. The operator needs to know when he can or cannot trust the bean probe. Other factors to consider are that smaller batches may require less airflow, slower drum speed, lower charge temperatures, and, of course, lower gas settings.

It's tempting to apply the same bean-temperature profile to all batch sizes of a given bean. In theory, it's possible. In practice, it's nearly impossible to precisely adjust a roaster's initial thermal energy and subsequent gas settings to track the same profile for a variety of batch sizes. It's probably wiser to accept a unique profile for each batch size. (Please note: Many roasters believe they are tracking the same profile perfectly with several different batch sizes. However, if their bean probes were to provide accurate bean-temperature readings during the first 2 minutes of every batch, they would likely witness variations they didn't realize existed.)

· 12 ·

Measuring
Results

To produce consistent roasts, one must measure results. Every roaster should roast with a bean probe, measure the weight loss of every batch, and use a refractometer to verify roast development. These measurement tools are affordable and easy to use. There is no excuse to not use them.

All About Bean Probes

The bean-temperature probe is the most important measurement device one can use while roasting. That said, your bean probe's reading is always playing catch-up with the beans, and it gives merely an approximation of average surface temperatures in the bean pile. It's also important to understand that bean-probe readings are not consistent from one machine to another. Probes installed in two different machines may read, for example, 20°F (11°C) apart at first crack, yet they may both be working properly.

Choosing a Probe

One may measure temperature with a Resistance Temperature Device (RTD) or a thermocouple. RTDs operate based on how changes in temperature alter the electrical resistance of metals in the probe. RTDs are more accurate but slower, more expensive,[13] and more fragile than thermocouples. Thermocouples function based on how two different metals in the probe generate a voltage in response to a temperature gradient.

For their combination of cost, accuracy, and responsiveness, I recommend that roasters use a Type K or Type J thermocouple. I also recommend choosing the smallest-practical sheath diameter to optimize probe responsiveness.[32] Beware that if a probe is too thin, the movement and weight of the beans may damage it during roasting. In very large machines with heavy bean loads, operators must use a slower-responding, large-diameter probe. For most small roasters, a 3-mm diameter probe is a good choice.

Installing a Probe

A bean probe must be fully immersed in the bean pile to provide the most accurate temperature information. If a probe contacts too much air relative to beans, its accuracy will suffer.

Install a bean probe where it will be immersed in the heart of the bean pile as it rotates. If you imagine the front of a roaster as a clock face, and the drum rotates clockwise, that spot is usually between the *7* and the *8* (closer to the *7*) and approximately 3–4 inches (7–10 cm) from the drum's inner edge. If the drum were rotating counterclockwise, the spot would be between the *4* and the *5*.

A small-diameter bean probe in a Lilla roaster

You must install the probe deep enough such that the length of shaft immersed in the bean pile is at least 6–10 times the probe's diameter.[13] If the probe interferes with the rotating drum's baffles, it might be all right to bend the probe (double-check first with the probe manufacturer), but be careful that you don't kink the sheath. I recommend bending the thermocouple such that the bulk of its shaft runs in the direction of the local bean motion, to minimize wear on the probe.

Weight Loss

While bean color and final bean temperature are useful indicators of roast degree, they don't provide insight into the bean core's development. To measure whole-bean, not just surface, development, I recommend calculating the percentage of weight lost from each batch.

To measure weight loss, weigh the beans before and after roasting, prefer-

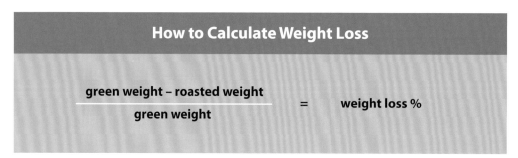

How to Calculate Weight Loss

$$\frac{\text{green weight} - \text{roasted weight}}{\text{green weight}} = \text{weight loss \%}$$

ably to a resolution of at least .01 lb or .005 kg. The difference is the weight loss. Divide the weight loss by the green-coffee weight to derive the weight-loss percentage.

Knowing a roast's weight-loss percentage helps a roaster determine how well she is penetrating the bean core during roasting. For example, if one roasts two batches of a coffee to the same roast color and the first batch loses 15.0% of its weight, while the second batch loses 14.5%, the first batch is more developed. Assuming one roasts to a consistent color every batch, the weight-loss measurement offers useful and immediate feedback about roast development.

One should not attempt to apply weight-loss data from one bean type to another, due to differences in initial moisture content and other factors. Even when comparing roasts of the same bean type, one must be certain the green coffee's moisture content did not change between batches. For example, suppose in early November you roast a batch of a newly arrived Kenyan coffee and its weight loss is 14.8%. After storing the green coffee for a month in burlap sacks, you roast the last batch of the lot in mid-December. Despite following the same roast profile, the coffee yields a weight loss of only 14.0%. Why? Because the beans lost moisture during storage in the warehouse's cool, dry winter air.

Measuring Roast Degree

Various devices exist to measure the roast degree of coffee. Typically, the device user prepares a sample of roasted beans on a tray, places it in the machine, and receives a number representing the sample's roast degree. She then repeats the process with a ground sample of the coffee. The difference between the reading of the whole-bean and ground sample is the "spread." A narrower spread is meant to indicate a more evenly roasted bean.

In my experience, the way in which a user prepares a sample unduly influences the readings of some of these machines. For example, several times I've witnessed two experienced users prepare samples from a roast batch and receive different results from the same machine. The grind size and smoothness of the sample surface, among other factors, may alter the roast-degree reading.

I don't know what caused all of the variations I've experienced, but if the results are so variable among experienced users, I question the benefit of these machines. Given their potentially inconsistent data, plus the cost of buying the machine and wasting grounds to take a reading, I prefer to measure roast degree using a combination of final bean temperature, visual cues (bean color and texture), and weight-loss calculations.

Verification of Development Using a Refractometer

A coffee's extraction potential depends on roast development. Inadequate development will limit a bean's solubility, and hence its extraction. For example, let's say you roast two batches of a coffee to the same color and pull several espresso shots from each batch using identical inputs (temperature, time, ground weight, shot weight, and so on). If batch A consistently yields extractions near 19.0% and batch B averages 16.5%, batch A is almost certainly more developed than batch B. In such a case a refractometer offers objective verification of roast development.

The coffee refractometer has had more impact on coffee quality than any other invention in decades.

· 13 ·

Sample Roasting

All the principles of roasting on a large machine apply to sample roasting. Many owners of small roasting businesses have commented to me that they usually prefer the coffee made from their sample roasters to that made from their production roasts. That's not surprising, because sample roasters often have more power than small shop roasters, relative to the small batches they roast. A high ratio of gas power to batch size facilitates good development. However, most sample roasters have rudimentary controls, making consistency challenging.

Most older sample roasters offer the user only two controls: a manual knob to control the gas setting and an environmental probe. To make the most of such a machine, I recommend using the following procedure:

1. Stabilize the roasting environment at one particular temperature between 410°F–420°F (210°C–216°C), with the drum empty before charging.
2. Charge the coffee and do not change the gas setting.

Sample roasting

Six-barrel sample roaster

3. About 30 seconds before first crack, decrease the gas by approximately 40%. If this produces a very fast roast (less than 8 minutes) or a very slow one (more than 13 minutes, which is slow for a sample roaster), try changing the pre-roast stabilization temperature.
4. Aim for a 9–11 minute roast.

This strategy is simplistic but often yields surprisingly good results and consistency, given that the operator doesn't have much feedback or control while roasting.

Ideally, one should use a bean probe when sample roasting. Beware, though, that in many sample roasters it may be difficult or impossible to immerse the probe in the bean pile sufficiently to produce reliable temperature readings. If your sample roaster doesn't already have a *manometer* or other precise indicator of gas setting, I recommend investing in one. When using a sample roaster with adequate controls (bean probe, air probe, manometer, and so on), one can roast exactly as one would in a production machine, though one might consider using faster profiles with a sample roaster.

Cupping

Cupping is a systematic, somewhat standardized, method of evaluating coffee. Cupping requires no special equipment, is easy to replicate, and is accessible to anyone with a grinder and hot water, whether she is a coffee farmer in Ethiopia or he is a barista in New York. The process allows the cupper to brew small samples and compare them rapidly, going back and forth between cups as needed.

Cupping

How to Cup

The following is one effective version of standard cupping procedure. You may prefer to vary some of the details, but, regardless of your exact method, please treat every sample identically.

You will need: a hot-water kettle, cupping bowls or glasses with capacity of 6–10 oz (175–300 ml), cupping spoons, one spittoon per cupper, cupping forms or notepads, a timer, a grinder, a gram scale, and a few tall cups filled with water for rinsing spoons.

1. Boil a kettle containing more water than you will require.
2. Plan to taste as many as five or six samples, but ideally no more than that, in one session.*
3. Grind 10.0 g** of each coffee into an 8–10 oz (235–295 ml) widemouthed glass or ceramic cup. The grind should be medium–fine, similar to an appropriate manual-pourover grind; I recommend using a refractometer to determine the grind setting that produces your target extraction.
4. Sniff the fragrance of each sample. The most volatile aromatics, or those with the lowest boiling points, make up the dry aroma. Its intensity indicates the freshness of the roast and grind.
5. Once the kettle boils, remove its cover and allow the water to cool to 204°F–205°F (96°C), before pouring. (This usually takes about 45–60 seconds, or longer for larger kettles.)
6. Tare the first cup on the gram scale.
7. Start a timer.
8. Pour 170 g of water over the grounds such that the water's turbulence mixes and wets all the grounds. (Alternatively, use 7 g of grounds and 120 g of water in smaller cups.)
9. Bring your nose close to the coffee's surface and sniff. At this moment, the coffee offers the most aroma. Don't miss it.
10. Pour the other cups in quick succession, taking a moment to smell each one.
11. After 4 minutes have elapsed, "break the crust" of the cups in the order in which they were poured. To break the crust, dip the bowl of a cupping spoon halfway into the coffee, push aside the crust of grounds with the back of the spoon, and bring your nose close to the surface of the coffee without touching the grounds with your nose. Sniff the aromatics released as you break each crust.
12. Inhale slowly and deeply as you break each crust. Long, slow inhalations provide better aroma detection than short sniffs.[33] Take notes on your impressions.
13. After breaking all the crusts, remove the grounds, foam, and oils from the surface of the cups. An efficient method is to skim the surface using two cupping spoons simultaneously.
14. At 9:00, begin tasting the coffees. Dip a cupping spoon just below the surface of the coffee, raise it to your lips, and vigorously slurp the coffee, spraying it throughout your mouth. (Many cuppers prefer to wait for the coffee to cool further before sampling. I recommend tasting the coffees at the highest temperature you can comfortably tolerate, but not before 9 minutes have elapsed. It's advantageous to taste the coffee at a wide range of temperatures.)

---

* Some circumstances require many more than six samples, but when possible, limit the number; the palate loses sensitivity with each successive cup tasted, a phenomenon known as "taste adaptation."[33]

**These days, scales with resolution of .01 g are readily available online for USD 20. Please use such a scale to weigh grounds for cupping. Using a scale with resolution of 0.5 g or more can easily invalidate the results of a cupping due to extraction variability among different cups.

15. Focus on the coffee's aromatics, mouthfeel, flavor, and other impressions. Take notes.
16. Spit out the coffee. If you're not sampling too many coffees in the session, consider swallowing the occasional spoonful. Swallowing promotes *retronasal olfaction*[33] and ensures the cupper exposes his farthest-back taste buds to a sample.
17. Move on to the other coffees, slurping and spitting as needed to get sufficient impressions of all of them. There is no need to "cleanse the palate" between each slurp, but swishing some water in the mouth every few minutes may help refresh the taste buds and forestall palate fatigue.
18. Record copious notes while cupping.
19. Take a break for a few minutes. Slurp and spit the coffees again when they are lukewarm.
20. Allow the coffees to cool to room temperature, about 15–30 minutes, and repeat the process of slurping and spitting. You will find the coffees offer much new information after they have cooled.

Cupping Recommendations

I recommend cupping coffees the day after they're roasted, if possible. Cupping should always be done blindly, meaning the cuppers do not know what coffees they are tasting. To set up a blind cupping, label the cup bottoms before pouring the water, or have someone who will not be tasting the coffee arrange the cups. Everyone is susceptible to bias, so blind cupping is the only way to ensure a fair evaluation of coffees. Blind cupping is also the most effective way to learn and to improve one's tasting skills.

Crusts ready to be broken

High-pressure blind cupping

The one unbreakable rule of cupping is that all coffee samples must be treated identically; all cups should have the same grind setting, ground coffee weight, water weight, steeping time, and so on. One who executes a cupping properly can be confident that all the perceived differences in the cups are inherent in the coffees and are not artifacts of the cupping process. Something as simple as pouring 10 g more water into one cup than another (easy to do, as you'll find if you weigh your filled cups) may noticeably alter a sample's extraction, flavor, and body.

One may also cup to test the effect of changing one variable, such as grind setting, variety of green coffee, roast profile, brewing temperature, and so on. As long as the only difference among the cups is the variable being tested, the cupping will be valid and offer useful information.

I recommend using a refractometer to equilibrate your cupping extraction level with your typical brewing extraction. For example, if you prepare your espresso and drip brews at 20% extraction, you should cup at 20% as well. However, I recommend cupping at lower brew strength than you likely prefer. Brew strengths of approximately 1.15%–1.35% are strong enough to give a cupper a fair impression of a coffee's body but dilute enough to offer excellent flavor clarity. Most professionals prefer drinking stronger brews, but additional brew strength may hamper one's ability to discern subtleties in a coffee. To me, cupping isn't about maximizing enjoyment as much as it is about optimizing one's ability to analyze coffees (though I hope it's enjoyable too).

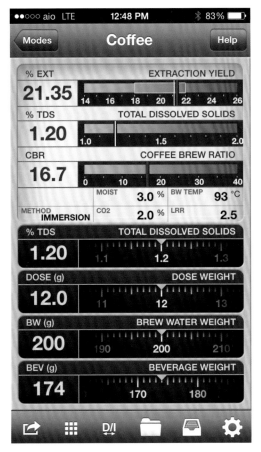

Extraction measurements of a recent cupping

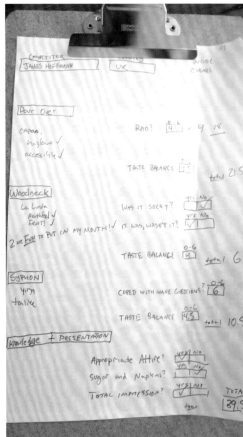

Judge Babinski's score sheet

The Phases of Cupping

Each phase of a cupping offers a different perspective on its samples. Take full advantage of all the phases to get as much information as you can about the coffees on the table.

Dry Aroma, or Fragrance

Smelling the dry grounds may indicate whether a sample was overroasted or if the roaster used insufficient airflow. The fragrance may also hint at the coffee's bouquet and fruit notes, as well as some defects due to age, *ferment,* or under-ripe cherries.

Wet Aroma

The sooner you can smell coffee after the water contacts the grounds, the better. Release of aromatics is correlated with temperature, and coffee offers its peak aroma when it is hottest. I find this moment also provides the best opportunity to sense underdevelopment. If the aroma is savory or vegetal upon wetting the grounds, development is probably insufficient.

Tasting the Coffee When It Is Hot

When slurping coffee, abandon all politeness. In cupping, loud slurping is a badge of honor. (In fact, slurping loudly once blew my cover at a public cupping where I had hoped to not be recognized as a coffee professional.) Vigorous spraying aerates the coffee in the mouth, which improves retronasal olfaction by increasing the quantity and speed of aroma delivery to the nose.

Even when coffee is in one's mouth, the nose does most of the sensing. The tongue is able to sense only the five tastes of bitter, sour, sweet, salty, and umami. The nose, on the other hand, can discriminate among thousands of aromatic compounds, often in concentrations as low as a few parts per billion. Each coffee has a unique aromatic signature made up of hundreds of volatile aromatics. It's this particular combination of volatiles that potentially allows a cupper to discriminate between similar coffees with a single sniff. Retronasal olfaction, not tongue-tasting, provides the majority of one's impressions while cupping.

Tasting the Coffee When It Is Cool

Hot coffee is more acidic than cold coffee. Cupping coffee when hot provides the best opportunity to evaluate acidity, brightness, sweetness, balance, and many other qualities. However, acidity also acts like a fog cover, obscuring the view of many subtleties hiding beneath. Once coffee cools and much of the acidity dissipates, other qualities, especially green-coffee defects and certain roast effects, become clearer.

How to Interpret Cupping Results

This is a book about roasting, not about green-coffee evaluation. Discussing how to analyze green coffee is beyond its scope and, frankly, is not my forte. I will focus here only on how aspects of a roast profile translate to the cupping table. To do this requires the cupper to discriminate between which cup characteristics represent a bean's unique traits and which are predominantly artifacts of the roast curve. This skill requires extensive experience and, preferably, tutelage under a skilled roaster.

A combination of a coffee's green-bean chemistry and its roast contribute to every flavor in the cup, but for practical purposes one may segregate some cup attributes based on which had a greater influence. For example, when a coffee tastes grassy, savory, baked, burnt, or smoky, it's reasonable to view those traits as generic results of roasting mistakes. Roasting also heavily influences a cup's balance of acid, sweetness, caramel, and bittersweet flavors. Alternatively, a coffee's intrinsic personality shows itself in its particular aromatic signature and specific flavor notes, such as "raspberry," "lavender," "earthy," and so on. Arguably, lighter roasting allows a cupper to identify a greater number of a bean's unique traits.

The following table is a sampling of common cup qualities caused by roasting mistakes, and how to fix them.

I realize it may be difficult to relate to the flavor descriptors above, as one cupper might use terms to describe a given quality that are different from what another cupper would use. The table should make more sense with time if you use it as a reference and experiment with its recommendations. If you would

Flavor	What it means	Most likely remedies
Savory or brothy	Very underdeveloped	Sharply steepen the early stages of the roast curve by charging hotter or using more gas during the first minutes of the roast. Ensure the development-time ratio is greater than 20%.
Grassy	Mildly underdeveloped	Moderately steepen the early roast curve. Ensure the development-time ratio is greater than 20%.
Sour or underripe fruit	Inner bean is developed but too light	Gently steepen the early roast curve or possibly roast darker. Ensure cupping extraction was greater than 19%, as under-extraction may also cause sourness. Ensure the development-time ratio is greater than 20%.
Paper, cardboard, or straw	Baked	Smooth out the bean progression. Ensure the ROR curve did not ever flatten or drop sharply.
Smoky (but not a dark roast)	Insufficient airflow late in the roast	Increase the airflow, especially during the last third of the roast.
Soggy cereal	Either insufficient airflow or a jagged ROR curve	Test the airflow during the early and middle stages of the roast. If it is adequate, smooth the ROR curve. Ensure that gas delivery is steady and not fluctuating. (This requires a manometer.)
Char	Burning due to overheated drum	Consider roasting more slowly or reshaping the roast curve to accommodate lower peak gas settings.
Bile or tangy, smoky	Insufficient airflow	Increase airflow. (I've found this quality most frequently in recirculation roasters and in light, very-low-airflow roasts. This quality morphs into a more general "smoky" aroma upon darker roasting.)
Bittersweet	Slightly overroasted	Unless you're seeking this quality in your coffee, roast lighter.
Acrid	Definitely overroasted	Roast lighter. Also check for adequate airflow late in the roast.
Carbonized	Ridiculously overroasted	Roast a lot lighter. Improve your palate. Perhaps look for a different job.

like to experience these traits and remedies firsthand, consider trying the "Roast Defect Training Kit" (available from www.scottrao.com in early 2015).

Here is an example of how to use the table's recommendations: Suppose you are cupping a light roast of a Kenyan coffee with notes of lemon, blueberry, grass, cardboard, and smoke, and you find the coffee a little more acidic than you would prefer. I would categorize the lemon and blueberry flavors as inherent bean traits, whereas the grass, cardboard, and smoke flavors are roast artifacts. The grassiness indicates you could have developed the coffee a little more. Increasing development will also likely curb the excess acidity. The smokiness indicates a need for more airflow, and the cardboard betrays a flattening of the ROR curve.

To improve the roast, I would recommend the following:

- Charge hotter or with more gas to jumpstart development.
- Increase the airflow, especially during the last third of the roast, to prevent smokiness.
- Alter the gas settings to create a smoothly declining ROR curve and prevent baking.

<h1>· 15 ·</h1>

<h1>Roasting, Brewing, and Extraction</h1>

How dark should you roast? I can't answer that question for you, but if you master roast development and coffee extraction, you might find that your preferred roast degree gets lighter. Inadequate development and extraction often yield sharp- or sour-tasting coffee, causing roasters to roast darker to tone down those qualities. Darker roasting will diminish these undesirable flavors, but it will also decrease sweetness and aroma while increasing weight loss. The goal of this chapter is to help roasters roast lighter, if they desire to, by learning to identify development and extraction problems.

Testing Roast Development

The lighter one roasts, the more challenging it is to fully develop the bean centers. When a roaster has difficulty developing a coffee, he will often choose to roast darker to improve the odds of good development. Ideally, when struggling with development, a roaster should figure out how to increase development at the desired roast degree, not roast darker to cover up inadequate development.*

If you would like to test and calibrate your roast development, especially if you are not regularly extracting above 19% with ease, consider purchasing a "control" coffee that is definitely well developed. I recommend against buying a lightly roasted coffee from one of today's popular third-wave roasters as your control, as few of them fully develop their coffee with consistency. Instead, I recommend using a trick I learned from Vince Fedele of VST Inc, inventor of the coffee refractometer: Buy a light-to-medium roast from Illy. Illy's choice of green coffee or roast may not match your taste, but you can be assured of fully developed beans. (If you'd like other suggestions for obtaining fully developed roasts, feel free to email me at scottrao@gmail.com.) Your coffee's extractions should approximate those of the control coffee, although some well-developed, very light roasts may extract a percentage point or so lower than the control beans.

Calibrating Extraction

Much as poor development may lead one to roast darker, habitual underextraction may also influence a roaster's choice of roast degree. Underextraction often produces sour-tasting coffee, especially when the beans are brewed as espresso. Roasters who don't realize they are underextracting often try to decrease acid-

---

* I don't advocate roasting lightly for its own sake. Until a roaster figures out how to fully develop beans at a particular roast degree, he should roast a little darker to ensure good development. I believe a caramelly medium roast is preferable to a sour, vegetal, underdeveloped light roast.

ity by roasting darker or extending the roast time after first crack, baking their coffee along the way. These roasters will produce better coffee if they ensure they are judging roasts brewed at proper extractions levels. I recommend measuring your extractions frequently with a refractometer to be certain you are evaluating roasts at your grinder's optimal extraction level. Ideal extractions for most brewing methods are usually in the range of 19%–22%, depending on the grinder and the sharpness of its burrs. Please see my ebook *Espresso Extraction: Measurement and Mastery* (available from all Amazon.com websites) for an in-depth discussion of this topic.

As a practical benchmark, aim for a minimum extraction of 19.5% when brewing espresso with a 50%, or 1:2, brewing ratio (i.e., the dry dose is half of the shot weight). For example, if you use 18 g of grounds to produce a 36 g shot, the extraction should be 19.5% or higher.

If your roasts do not regularly yield 19.5% when you use a 1:2 brewing ratio, first ensure that your roast development is adequate (ideally, by comparing your coffee's extractions with those of a control coffee). If you are confident in the roast development, then inappropriate brewing-water chemistry, low grind quality, or poor brewing technique may be limiting extraction. Substandard brewing water, such as water that has very high total dissolved solids (TDS) or hard water that has been artificially softened, may limit extraction because it is a poor solvent. Low grind quality, usually due to small or dull burrs, may produce too many fines and *boulders,* which also decreases extraction. If you find that your extractions are inconsistent, even when pulling shots from the same roast batch, improper technique is probably hindering you.

I've had some amazing espresso in Andy's kitchen.

Roasting for Espresso

Most roasters roast their espresso blends darker than their other coffees. That's understandable, given that the vast majority of espresso shots end up in milky drinks. Most light roasts either don't have the heft to balance several ounces of milk or they are too acidic to complement the flavor of milk. Other than potentially roasting darker, particularly for shots intended for milk-based drinks, I do not think roasters should make any other adjustments when roasting for espresso.

The goal when roasting for any brewing method should be to create the desired balance of sweetness and acidity while maximizing development. If a roaster follows the roasting recommendations in this book and extracts espresso properly, he will likely find that his preferred roast for straight espresso (i.e., served without milk) is identical, or nearly so, to his chosen roast for filter coffee and other brewing methods.

As noted in the previous section, poor development and underextraction often have undue influences on roasting decisions. In the case of espresso, during the two decades before the arrival of the coffee refractometer, two concurrent trends in specialty coffee conspired to decrease development and extraction: lighter roasting and ristretto espresso. As the more progressive roasters adopted lighter roasting styles, underdevelopment became rampant. Simultaneously, underextraction became the norm with the rising popularity of ristretto-style espresso in third-wave shops.*

The coffee refractometer has provided roasters and baristi with an objective measurement of their extractions and has all but eliminated the third-wave obsession with underextracted ristretto shots. The next step is for roasters to improve their understanding of how to develop roasts efficiently. My hope is that the information in this book, especially Chapter 10, "The Three Commandments of Roasting," helps roasters improve their bean development.

Blending

While the current trend is to serve single-origin coffee, the historical norm has been to brew blends of various beans. Blending allows a roaster to create a unique flavor profile that does not exist in any one bean. Alternatively, blending also enables a roaster to offer a more consistent flavor profile throughout the year; substitute coffees as needed based on cost, availability, or flavor; and invest in the marketing of a blend's name. Proponents argue that blending provides consistency, while skeptics see it as a way for roasters to save money or mislead consumers. For example, coffee labeled "Kona blend" may legally contain only 10% of beans from Kona.

Inconsistent roasting, continual changes in green coffee's quality and flavor throughout the year, and variations in harvest quality make blending inherently challenging. Simply put, there are too many moving parts to blend by

---

* Two notable exceptions are Nordic roasters, who have always roasted lightly, generally with skill, and Italian roasters, who have always roasted a little darker and extracted to reasonable levels. Those two groups largely avoided following the dual trends of underextracting and underdeveloping.

formula. I recommend blending based on taste but acknowledge that results will never be perfectly consistent.

Roasters often debate the merits of blending before roasting (known as "pre-blending") versus blending after roasting ("post-blending"). I believe that both methods can produce excellent results if done properly, though I personally prefer post-blending by taste.

I recommend the following procedure for post-blending:

1. Set up a cupping of all potential blend components, using relatively large samples. Brew with a ratio of perhaps 20 g of grounds to 320 g of water.
2. Spoon portions of each brewed component into an empty cup in the ratio you'd like to test. For example, to test a blend of three equal components, put 1 spoonful of liquid from each brew into the blending cup. For a 50/25/25 blend, use 2 spoonfuls of the first component and 1 spoonful each of the other components.
3. Taste the blend and repeat the process, adjusting the ratio of spoonfuls as you go.
4. Once you've settled on a blend, brew it as you normally would to confirm the results from the cupping table.

If you choose to pre-blend, I recommend meeting all of the following criteria to ensure good results:

- Blend the green coffees a few days before roasting to equilibrate their moisture contents.
- Use only beans of very similar size and density.
- Use only beans of the same processing type (for example, either washed or natural).

· 16 ·

Storing
Roasted Coffee

F reshly roasted coffee contains approximately 2% carbon dioxide and other gases by weight. Pressure within the beans causes the gases to *desorb* (i.e., to be released) slowly, over many weeks' time after roasting. During the first 12 hours or so after roasting, the internal bean pressure is high enough to prevent significant amounts of oxygen from entering a bean's structure. Thereafter, oxidation causes staling of the coffee and degradation of its flavor.

A bean's gas content, internal pressure, and rate of outgassing are all affected by the roast method. Roasting hotter or darker produces more gas, greater internal bean pressure, and a more expanded cell structure, with larger pores. These factors lead to faster gas desorption and accelerated staling after roasting. While I don't think one should change roasting styles simply to increase roasted coffee's shelf life, it's useful to understand that darker roasts degas and stale more quickly than lighter roasts.

Roast development also affects the rate of degassing. If a bean is underdeveloped, parts of its cellulose structure will remain tough and nonporous, trapping gases in its inner chambers. A noticeable lack of outgassing in bagged, roasted coffee may indicate underdevelopment.

Several options exist for storing roasted beans, and each has unique pros and cons:

· Unsealed containers
· Valve bags
· Vacuum-sealed valve bags
· Nitrogen-flushed valve bags
· Airtight bags
· Nitrogen-flushed, pressurized containers
· Freezing

Unsealed containers: Beans stored in an unsealed bag or other air-filled container (such as a bucket with a lid) stale quickly. Ideally, consume such coffee within 2–3 days of roasting.

Valve bags: Bags with one-way valves are the standard in the specialty-coffee industry. Such bags allow gas to escape but generally prevent new air from entering. Coffee held in such bags will taste fresh for a couple of weeks. The most noticeable change in the coffee after a few weeks in a valve bag is loss of carbon dioxide and aroma. The CO_2 loss will be especially noticeable during espresso extraction as a lack of crema.

Vacuum-sealed valve bags: Vacuum sealing greatly limits oxidation of coffee in a valve bag, slowing its flavor degradation.

An upstart roastery's coffee in a valve bag

Nitrogen-flushed valve bags: Flushing a valve bag with nitrogen decreases potential oxidation to almost nil. Valve bagging limits coffee's oxidation but has minimal effect on the loss of internal, pressurized gases. Upon opening a valve bag after several days or weeks of storage, the beans stale much faster than fresh, just-roasted coffee would, because they lack gas pressure to repel oxygen. For example, coffee stored in a valve bag for 1 week will taste fresh upon opening the bag but within a day will degrade almost as much as it would have had it spent the week in an unsealed bag.

Airtight bags: Few roasters use airtight bags anymore. Such bags limit oxidation, but bean outgassing causes the bags to puff up, making their storage and handling inconvenient.

Nitrogen-flushed, pressurized containers: This is the most effective packaging option. Nitrogen flushing prevents oxidation, and pressurizing the container (usually a can) prevents outgassing. Storing the container at a cool temperature (the cooler, the better) slows staling, allowing a coffee to taste fresh for months after roasting.

Freezing: Although it still has its skeptics, freezing has proven itself to be very effective for long-term coffee storage. Freezing decreases oxidation rates by more than 90% and slows the movement of volatiles.[34] There is no need to worry about the moisture in freshly roasted coffee actually freezing, as it is bound to the cellulose matrix, which makes it nonfreezable.[35] The best way to freeze beans is to put a single serving (whether for a pot or a cup) into an airtight package, such as a Ziploc® bag. Remove the package from the freezer and allow the beans to warm to room temperature before opening the package and grinding the beans.

· 17 ·

Choosing Machinery

Selecting a roasting machine is a long-term commitment, and I hope readers do their homework before buying a machine. Most small roasters, especially first-time buyers, don't have the experience to evaluate machines properly, so if that's you, I recommend seeking expert advice before making what is probably your company's largest investment. You must choose carefully because the majority of machines on the market today will limit your coffee's quality or consistency, though their sales representatives may neglect to tell you that.

Features to Consider when Selecting a Roaster

Every roasting company has its unique list of needs and preferences when choosing a roaster, such as aesthetics, machine footprint, cost, and so on. While I can't comment on those company-specific requirements, I offer the following technical recommendations to help you choose a roaster.

Capacity

First, decide how much roasting capacity you need. Second, use a manufacturer's stated capacity as a starting point and look up a machine's BTU rating to estimate what its realistic capacity might be. Finally, given that every machine will have different heat-transfer efficiency, I recommend that you contact a few users of a given machine to ask about their typical batch sizes and roast times. Using those three pieces of information, you should have a good sense of the machine's realistic capacity.

Configuration

A roasting machine's configuration probably has the greatest effect on the quality of coffee that it can produce. As I'm sure you've gathered by now, I recommend single-pass roasters over recirculation roasters, despite the latter's energy efficiency. I also recommend an indirectly heated drum, or a double drum, over a standard flame-on-drum design. A single-pass roaster with a double drum or indirectly heated drum will maximize your chances of producing great coffee and minimize potential flavor taints due to bean-surface burning or a smoky roasting environment.

The Drum

If you buy a classic drum roaster with a flame-on-drum configuration, I recommend choosing a machine with a carbon-steel drum. Contrary to popular belief, most old, German "cast-iron roasters" have carbon-steel drums, not cast-iron drums. Those machines and many others often have cast-iron faceplates, drum spokes, and drum paddles, but steel drums. I have seen one machine with

Single-walled steel drum

a cast-iron drum (a small, newer roaster manufactured in Taiwan) and one machine with a sheet-iron drum, but every other machine I've ever seen has had a steel drum.

Most roasting drums are made of carbon steel, but some manufacturers have recently begun building machines with stainless-steel drums; this seems reasonable, but I don't have enough experience with them to have an opinion about their performance. Stainless steel drums may develop hot spots more easily than mild carbon steel ones, but that's probably not a serious concern, given the drum's rotation and an adequate thickness.

Airflow

I've come across few roasters with inadequate airflow but several machines with poor airflow adjustment mechanisms. Ideally, your exhaust fan's RPM should be adjustable in minute, stepless increments. Subtler airflow adjustments will produce smoother roast profiles. Machines with two or three discreet airflow settings, usually controlled manually by a damper, are acceptable but limiting. Not only are the settings usually too far apart, forcing the machine operator to compromise and choose a suboptimal setting, but the large shifts in airflow when adjusting settings may cause undesirable jumps in rates of convective heat transfer.

Some machines use one fan to draw air through the roasting drum and cooling bin. I do not recommend most of these machines; they inhibit management of the drum temperature while beans cool between batches, and they limit airflow options early in a batch if the operator is roasting and cooling simultaneously. Most of these roasters also tend to cool beans too slowly, as the single fan is rarely as powerful as other machines' dedicated cooling fans.

Full batches should cool to near room temperature in 4 minutes or less. I recommend testing a roaster's cooling efficiency before committing to it. Rapid cooling prevents baked flavors and loss of sweetness and allows more precise termination of the roasting process.

Gas Control

Beyond having adequate gas power, a roasting machine should offer steplessly adjustable gas settings. Virtually every larger machine of 30 kg capacity or greater offers stepless gas adjustment, but many smaller machines offer either stepped gas adjustment or a mere two or three settings. Stepless adjustment offers much more flexibility when an operator is trying to replicate desired roast profiles across a variety of batch sizes. I've challenged several manufacturers about why they offer limited gas control on smaller machines while they offered stepless adjustment on their larger machines. They have usually replied with vague references to smaller machines having "different physics," whatever that means. So far, none have made a compelling argument for the benefit of lim-

Spelling aside, this is not the best way to adjust airflow.

ited gas control. I suspect that the real reason they offer limited burner control on their smaller machines is that such burners are substantially cheaper to produce, and the manufacturers want to remain price competitive in the small-machine market.

Drum Speed

Adjustable drum speed is probably the least important of the various roasting controls, but it can help fine-tune roasts. As a roast progresses, the beans expand, which changes the way they rotate in the drum. Small, incremental increases in drum RPM will maintain ideal rotation for uniform roasting as the beans expand. Adjustable drum speed is also useful when one is roasting a variety of batch sizes.

Data-Logging Software

Successful roasters today use everything from fully manual machines to fully automated machines. Regardless of how you feel about roasting technology, I recommend that you use, at the very least, a digital bean-temperature probe, a digital environmental probe, and a manometer or other indicator of gas pressure. If you are not using automated profiling software, I recommend using a data-logging aid such as Cropster® software to track and log roast profiles. Data-logging software offers real-time graphical feedback about roast progress, profile tracking, and, in the case of Cropster, the rate-of-rise curve, which is indispensable. These programs do not control the roaster, but they provide today's best option for real-time roasting feedback and record keeping.

Manometer

Automated Roast Profile

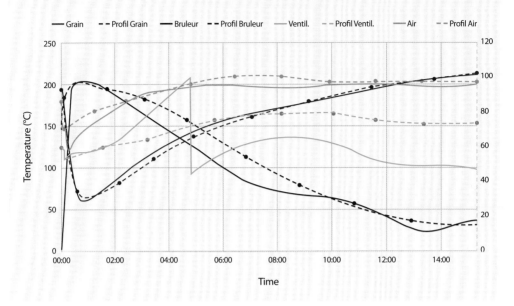

This brand of software usually tracks profiles better than most, but in this example, the software abruptly changed the exhaust fan RPM in a desperate attempt to stay on profile. Most profiling software seems to make similar, extreme adjustments at unpredictable times.

Be aware that upgrading a vintage roaster to work with modern technology will be an expensive headache. The chore of replacing older gear with digital probes, solenoid valves, variable-speed motors, and so on somehow always takes longer and costs much more than anyone expected. It's not unusual for the modifications to cost more than the roaster itself. If that sort of project doesn't appeal to you, consider buying a more modern machine.

Automated Profiling Software

While data-logging software tracks roasts but does not control a roaster, automated profiling software tracks and controls roasts via a feedback loop. These programs attempt to follow a "model" roast profile by controlling the gas and airflow during a roast. Whenever a roast does not track the model curve exactly, the software makes tiny adjustments, as often as multiple times per second, to stay on the curve. Profiling software works like a person driving a car: No one steers perfectly straight ahead; instead, one makes frequent microadjustments to steer as straight as possible.

While a well-designed automated system could theoretically roast more consistently than any human could, most of the systems on the market today do a poor job of reliably replicating roasting results. Despite sales departments' claims to the contrary, no off-the-shelf roasting software will keep your roast pinned to the intended profile every batch, at least not without some tricks that compromise coffee flavor. Often, when a batch drifts a little off course, software overreacts by drastically changing the gas setting or exhaust fan RPM to stay

A Joper with an afterburner (The afterburner is the stainless steel cylinder at the top left.)

on profile. In such a batch, the software may successfully track the profile, but the result in the cup will differ from what one would expect from the model profile.

You might not want to roast using automated profiling software, but if you can afford it, you might consider buying the software for purposes other than controlling roasts. Allowing the software to manage a roaster during the initial warm-up, between batches, and during the cool-down at the end of a roast session frees the machine operator to tend to other tasks, thereby increasing productivity. Depending on the software's proficiency, you might feel comfortable allowing it to manage certain phases of some roasts. Roast-profiling software also usefully catalogs past batches and profiles for future reference.

Pollution-Control Devices

When buying a roasting machine, you must decide whether you need a pollution-control device. Roasters most commonly use afterburners and occasionally use *electrostatic precipitators* or *wet scrubbers*.

Coffee roasting produces a long list of nasty emissions, many of which are carcinogenic, including volatile organic compounds, aldehydes, nitrogen compounds, sulfur compounds, and carbon monoxide. The particulate matter in smoke from roasters contributes to air pollution, and the odor of the emissions often bothers neighbors. Most jurisdictions do not require small roasters to use pollution-control devices, but without one, a roaster may run into problems with neighbors who file "nuisance complaints" about the roaster's smoke and smell. I had a long, stressful, and expensive conflict with the neighbors of my first roastery, even though I was roasting only 20 lb batches for 10 hours per week in the business district of a small town. My advice is to do your homework, find out what your local government requires, and try to figure out what your neighbors will accept before you install a roaster. A little research ahead of time may save you a lot of headaches later.

Roasters have two main choices of afterburner: *thermal oxidizer* or *catalytic oxidizer*. A thermal oxidizer heats a roaster's exhaust gases to approximately 1400°F (760°C) and retains the air for at least 0.4 second. It does a great job of eliminating smoke, volatile organic compounds, and odors but consumes a tremendous amount of fuel, often twice as much as its associated roasting machine. Catalytic oxidizers use a precious-metal catalyst that reacts with volatile organic compounds to produce CO_2 and water. The catalyst accelerates the reactions, allowing them to occur at lower temperatures. Catalytic oxidizers use less fuel than thermal oxidizers do, but they require periodic replacement of the catalyst and frequent cleaning to prevent back pressure that interferes with the roaster's airflow.

I've personally owned a pollution-control system consisting of a wet scrubber, electrostatic precipitator, and large box containing 500 lb of carbon pellets to absorb odors. Scrubbers and precipitators each remove particulate and odors from the air, and the carbon absorbs odors. While it's possible that those technologies have improved since my unpleasant experiences with them, I found they required a lot of cleaning and maintenance, created variable back pressure at the roaster, and were not as effective as an afterburner. If you buy a pollution-control device, I recommend sticking with the time-tested afterburner.

Parting Words

I've offered this book in hopes of helping roasters avoid some of the frustrations I experienced while learning to roast. I'd like the reader to view my recommendations as a set of successful methods learned over two decades of varied experience, not as a static system of rules.

While there are many legitimate approaches to roasting coffee, our industry has, until now, had little open discussion of a systematic approach. I hope, at the least, that this book is the beginning of that discussion.

Glossary

Acidity The sharpness, snap, sourness, or liveliness of coffee.

Afterburner A device that heats the exhaust air from a roaster in order to destroy particulate and odors.

Alkaloid Any of a group of organic, nitrogenous compounds that are physiologically active and usually bitter.

Aroma A quality that can be detected by the olfactory system.

Astringent Causing the mouth to pucker or feel dry upon ingestion.

Baked A roast defect that reduces coffee's sweetness and creates flat, papery, cereal-like flavors.

Bitter Having a sharp, pungent taste.

Body A beverage's weight or fullness as perceived in the mouth.

Boulders The largest coffee grounds in a particle size distribution.

Burlap A woven fabric made from fibers of the jute plant.

Caffeine A bitter, stimulating alkaloid.

Caramelization A complex series of sugar-browning reactions that creates numerous new compounds.

Carbonization The formation of carbon from an organic substance by pyrolysis.

Catalytic oxidizer An afterburner that uses a precious-metal catalyst to clean roasting exhaust at relatively low temperatures.

Cellulose A polysaccharide that is the main constituent of plant cell walls.

Chaff (silver skin) Part of the husk of the coffee seed (bean); released as beans expand during roasting.

Charge To load beans into the roasting chamber of a coffee-roasting machine.

Charge temperature The air temperature in an empty roasting machine just before a batch is loaded.

Cherry The fruit of a coffee tree.

Chlorogenic acid A polyphenol and antioxidant found in high concentration in coffee beans.

Cinnamon roast The lightest commercial roast; produced by dropping the beans during early first crack.

City roast A light roast, terminated during the latter stages of, or just after, first crack.

Coffea arabica The most widely planted and highest-quality commercial species of coffee plant, native to Ethiopia.

Coffea robusta (Coffea canephora) A hardy, but low-quality, commercial species of coffee plant native to sub-Saharan Africa. Robusta is the second-most-planted coffee species and yields coffee with approximately double the caffeine of arabica coffee.

Coffee-roasting machine A specialized oven that transfers heat to coffee beans in a stream of hot gas while continually mixing the beans to ensure they roast evenly.

Conduction The transfer of heat from one substance to another by direct contact.

Continuous roaster A high-yield roaster in which axial position, not time, determines bean temperature. Such roasters receive, roast, and discharge beans in a constant stream, as opposed to in batches.

Convection The transfer of heat by movement of a fluid.

Creosote A brown, oily liquid mixture of phenols and other organic compounds deposited in the exhaust ductwork of a coffee roaster.

Cupping A systematic, somewhat standardized, method of evaluating coffee.

Dark roast A smoky, bitter roast produced by discharging beans after the onset of second crack.

Desorb To cause the release of a substance from a surface.

Development The degree of breakdown of a roasted coffee bean's cellulose structure.

Double drum A coffee-roasting machine with a drum made of two concentric layers of metal separated by a gap several millimeters wide.

Drop To discharge beans from a coffee-roasting machine.

Drum roaster A coffee-roasting machine in which the beans are tumbled in a rotating, cylindrical drum.

Electrostatic precipitator A device that removes particulates from coffee-roasting exhaust by using a high-voltage electrostatic charge to cause the particles to stick to charged panels.

Endothermic A reaction requiring the absorption of heat energy.

Endothermic flash A phenomenon during first crack in which the release of water vapor from the inner beans causes the beans' surface temperatures to suddenly cool.

Environmental temperature The air temperature in a roasting machine.

Exothermic Releasing heat.

Facing Surface burning of a coffee bean; occurs late in a roast.

Ferment A green-coffee defect that is the result of chemical breakdown by microbes.

Fines Tiny cell-wall fragments produced by grinding coffee beans.

First crack A phase of coffee roasting characterized by loud, popping noises created by the release of pressure and water vapor from the inner beans.

Flavor The combined sensation of a substance's taste and aroma.

Fluid-bed roaster A drumless coffee-roasting machine in which beans are rotated and held aloft by a stream of hot gases.

French roast A dark, bittersweet roast produced by dropping a batch after oils begin to bleed from the bean surfaces.

Full city roast A medium roast dropped just before, or just after, the onset of second crack.

GrainPro A brand of hermetically sealed bags for storing agricultural products such as coffee beans.

Heat sink A medium that absorbs heat.

Hermetic Airtight.

High-yield roaster A very fast coffee-roasting machine that preserves an unusually high proportion of coffee's moisture and organic matter.

Italian roast The darkest commercial roast, which produces bitter, pungent, acrid coffee.

Light roast A roast level produced by dropping beans before, or just after, the end of first crack. Cinnamon and city roasts are light roasts.

Maillard reactions Chemical reactions between amino acids and reducing sugars that contribute to coffee's brown color and roasty flavors.

Manometer An instrument that uses a column of liquid to measure pressure.

Medium roast A roast dropped just before or just after the onset of second crack. Full city and Viennese are medium roasts.

Mouthfeel The in-mouth tactile sensations produced by a beverage.

Organic acid A carbon-containing compound with acidic properties.

Organoleptic Involving the sense organs.

Pungent A strong or sharp taste or smell; usually refers to spiciness.

Pyrolysis Decomposition caused by high temperatures.

Radiant In coffee roasting, a term describing the transfer of heat from one body to another in close proximity.

Rate of rise (ROR) The progression of bean temperature per unit time during a roast.

Reducing sugars In coffee roasting, sugars that donate electrons when reacting with amino acids in Maillard reactions.

Refractometer A device used to measure the refractive index of a solution. A coffee's refractive index directly relates to its density and concentration.

Respiration The exchange of gases by coffee beans with their environment.

Retronasal olfaction The smelling of odors through the mouth.

Roast profile A graphical representation of the progression of bean-probe temperature readings during a roast.

Scorching The burning of bean surfaces during the early stages of a roast.

Second crack A phase during a dark roast in which the release of CO_2 from the beans creates loud, popping noises.

Shrinkage The weight lost by coffee beans during roasting.

Soluble chemistry The coffee components that can be dissolved in water.

Specialty coffee Any reference to coffee, or the coffee business, related to the use of higher-quality arabica coffee beans.

Stack effect The movement of air out of a chimney due to differences in air density.

Taste The components of flavor perceived by the tongue.

Temperature gradient During roasting, the difference in temperature between a bean's core and its surface.

Thermal oxidizer See: afterburner

Thermometric lag The delay in a thermocouple's measurement of a substance's temperature.

Tipping Burn marks at the long ends, or "tips," of coffee beans.

Trigonelline A bitter alkaloid found in coffee; the methyl betaine of nicotinic acid.

Trowel A small scoop mounted in the faceplate of a coffee roaster for sampling beans during roasting.

Underdeveloped A term describing a part of a coffee bean's structure not sufficiently broken down by roasting.

Vacuum sealing A packaging method involving the removal of air before sealing.

Viennese roast A medium-dark roast produced by dropping beans just after the bleeding of oils from bean surfaces.

Volatile aromatic compounds Soluble gases that contribute to the aroma of coffee.

Water activity (a_w) The partial vapor pressure of water in a substance divided by the standard state partial vapor pressure of water.

Weight loss The decrease in weight of coffee beans during roasting.

Wet scrubber A device that passes a roaster's exhaust air through a spray of water to remove odors and particulates.

References

1. Johnson, B.; Standiford, K. and Johnson, W.M. (2008) *Practical Heating Technology*, 3rd ed. Cengage Learning, Independence, KY. 106–107.

2. Rivera, J. (2005) Alchemy in the roasting lab. *Roast.* March/April, 32–39.

3. www.coffeechemistry.com/caffeine/caffeine-in-coffee.html

4. Pittia, P.; Nicoli, M.C. and Sacchetti, G. (2007) Effect of moisture and water activity on textural properties of raw and roasted coffee beans. *Journal of Texture Studies.* 38, 116–134.

5. Petracco, M. (2005) Selected chapters in *Espresso Coffee: the Science of Quality,* edited by Illy, A. and Viani, R. Elsevier Applied Science, New York, NY.

6. Rivera, J. (2005) Alchemy in the roasting lab, part 2. *Roast.* May/June, 35–41.

7. Rivera, J. (2008) Under the microscope: the science of coffee roasting. *Roast.* May/June, 81–90.

8. Schenker, S. (2000) Investigations on the hot air roasting of coffee beans. Swiss Federal Institute of Technology, Zurich.

9. deleted

10. Probat Burns Inc. (2007) Technology with taste. 96th National Coffee Association Convention.

11. Wang, N. (2012) Physiochemical changes of coffee beans during roasting. Masters degree thesis. University of Guelph.

12. Barter, R. (2004) A short introduction to the theory and practice of profile roasting. *Tea & Coffee Trade Journal.* 68, 34–37.

13. www.teaandcoffee.net/0204/coffee.htm

14. http://www.thefreelibrary.com/_/print/PrintArticle.aspx?id=157587864

15. Ramey; Lambelet. (1982) A calorimetric study of self-heating in coffee and chicory. *International Journal of Food Science and Technology.* 17; 4, 451–460.

16. Clarke, R. and Vitzthum, O.G. (2001) *Coffee: Recent Developments.* Blackwell Science, Oxford, UK.

17. Duarte, S.M.; Bare, C.M.; Menezes, H.C.; Santos, M.H. and Gouvea, C.M. (2005) Effect of processing and roasting on the antioxidant activity of coffee brews. *Ciência e Tecnologia de Alimentos*. April–June, 387–393.

18. Illy, E. (2002) The complexity of coffee. *Scientific American*. June, 86–91.

19. McGee, H. (2004) *On Food and Cooking*. Scribner, New York, NY.

20. Lingle, T. (1996) *The Coffee Brewing Handbook*. Specialty Coffee Association of America, Long Beach, CA.

21. Ahmed, J. and Rahman, M.S. (2012) *Handbook of Food Process Design*. Wiley & Sons, West Sussex, UK.

22. Farid, M. (2010) *Mathematical modeling of food processing*. CRC Press, Boca Raton, FL.

23. Fabbri, A.; Cevoli, C.; Alessandrini, L. and Romani, S. (2011) Numerical model of heat and mass transfer during the coffee roasting process. *Journal of Food Engineering*. 105, 264–269.

24. http://cooking.stackexchange.com/questions/29926/what-temperature-does-the-maillard-reaction-occur

25. Dias, O.; Helena da Silva Brandão, E.; Landucci, F.L.; Koga-Ito, C.Y. and Jorge, A.O.C. (2007) Effects of *Coffea arabica* on *Streptococcus mutans* adherence to dental enamel and dentine. *Brazilian Journal of Oral Sciences*. 6, No. 23 (Oct–Dec), 1438–1441.

26. Adrian, J. and Francine, R. (1991) Synthesis and availability of niacin in roasted coffee. *Advances in Medical Biology*. 289, 49–59.

27. Farah, A.; Monitor, M.; Donangelo, C.M. and Leafy, S. (2008) Chlorogenic acids from green coffee extract are highly bioavailable in humans. *The Journal of Nutrition*. 2309–2315.

28. Schwartzberg, H. (2006) Improving industrial measurement of the temperature of roasting coffee beans. *Proceedings of the 21st International Conference on Coffee Science*.

29. Schwartzberg, H. (2004) Modelling exothermic heat generation during the roasting of coffee. *Proceedings of the 21st International Conference on Coffee Science*.

30. Eggers, R. and von Blittersdorff, M. (2005) Temperature field during the roasting and cooling of coffee beans. *Proceedings of 20th International Conference on Coffee Science*.

31. Shannon, K.S. and Butler, B.W. A Review of error associated with thermocouple temperature measurements in fire environments. USDA Forest Service.

32. Personal communication with Henry Schwartzberg.

33. Stuckey, Barb (2012) *Taste What You're Missing.* Simon & Schuster, New York, NY.

34. Sivetz, M. and Desrosier, N.W. (1979) *Coffee Technology.* Avi Publishing, Westport, CT.

35. Mateus, M.L.; Rouvet, M.; Gumy, J.C. and Liardon, R. (2007) Interactions of water with roasted and ground coffee in the wetting process investigated by a combination of physical determinations. *Journal of Agricultural and Food Chemistry.* 55, 2979–2984.

36. Frothier, I. (2014) Measuring water activity in high-end, specialty green coffee. *Roast.* Jan/Feb.

37. Trugo, L.C. and Marcie, R. (1985) The use of the mass detector for sugar analysis of coffee products. *Proceedings of the 11th ASIC Colloquium.*

38. Montessori, M.C.; Farah, A.S.; Calado, V. and Trugo, L.C. (2006) Correlation between cup quality and chemical attributes of Brazilian coffee. *Analytical, Nutritional, and Clinical Methods.* 98, 373–380.

Index

About the Author

Scott Rao has owned and operated cafes and has roasted coffee since 1994. When not writing books about coffee making, he does freelance consulting, specializing in coffee roasting and cafe startups. You can contact him at scottrao@gmail.com.